Complete Comprehension

Year 1

Contents

Year 1 overview	2
Introduction	4
Skills guide	14
Word meaning	14
Retrieval	16
Sequencing	18
Inference	20
Prediction	22
Teaching units and Progress checks	24

Schofield & Sims

Year 1 overview

Unit	Title	Focus	Page
Unit 1	**Starting School** (Picture comprehension)	Inference — Picture	page 24
Unit 2	**Our Senses** (Picture comprehension)	Retrieval — Picture	page 32
Unit 3	**Mary Had a Little Lamb** by Sarah Josepha Hale	Retrieval — Poetry	page 40
Unit 4	**Jack and Jill** (Traditional rhyme)	Word meaning — Poetry	page 48
Unit 5	**Snow Bear** by Tony Mitton	Inference — Fiction	page 56
Unit 6	**Can't You Sleep, Little Bear?** by Martin Waddell	Word meaning — Fiction	page 64
Unit 7	**Little Red** by Jo Gray	Inference — Fiction	page 72
Unit 8	**Wolves** by James Maclaine	Retrieval — Non-fiction	page 80
Unit 9	**The Three Little Pigs** by Jo Gray	Sequencing — Fiction	page 88
Unit 10	**The Three Little Pigs (Revolting Rhymes)** by Roald Dahl	Inference — Poetry	page 96
Unit 11	**Looking After Rabbits** by Fiona Patchett	Word meaning — Non-fiction	page 104
Unit 12	**The Pet** by Tony Bradman	Prediction — Poetry	page 112

Year 1 overview

Unit	Title	Skill	Page
Unit 13	**Chocolate Cake** by Michael Rosen	Inference — Poetry	page 120
Unit 14	**Chocolate Cake Recipe** by Jo Gray	Sequencing — Non-fiction	page 128
Unit 15	**Plant Facts** by Izzi Howell	Word meaning — Non-fiction	page 136
Unit 16	**Jack and the Beanstalk** by Jo Gray	Retrieval — Fiction	page 144
Unit 17	**My Two Grannies** by Floella Benjamin	Inference — Fiction	page 152
Unit 18	**Grandad Mandela** by Zazi, Ziwelene and Zindzi Mandela	Word meaning — Non-fiction	page 160
Progress check 1	**Bee Frog** by Martin Waddell	Mixed skills — Fiction	page 168
Progress check 2	**You Can't Take an Elephant on the Bus** by Patricia Cleveland-Peck	Mixed skills — Fiction	page 172
Progress check 3	**Seaside Towns** by Claire Hibbert	Mixed skills — Non-fiction	page 176

Introduction

Reading is one of the most important outcomes of a primary school education, and one of the most powerful skills we will ever master, as it is crucial for understanding the world around us. It is no exaggeration to say that the benefits of being an effective reader last a lifetime.

Complete Comprehension is a whole-school programme designed to equip pupils with everything they need to become strong, successful readers. The series, which comprises a book of lesson plans, teaching guidance and photocopiable resources for every year group from Year 1 to Year 6, breaks down the complex process of comprehension into separate **Comprehension skills** (see page 5).

The comprehension skills are signposted throughout the series through the use of child-friendly logos and graphics. Each teaching unit includes a photocopiable **Comprehension text** and a set of **Skills focus questions** that target a single skill, along with detailed guidance to support you, the teacher, to model the relevant skill in context using the **Let's try … questions**.

In addition, a **Skills guide** is provided at the end of this introduction (see page 14). It includes an in-depth **description** of each skill, and explains how the skills relate to each other. It also lists **strategies** to help you develop your pupils' familiarity with each skill and offers advice on how to deal with common difficulties. A selection of resources are also available to download from the Schofield & Sims website (www.schofieldandsims.co.uk/completecomprehension), including a selection of child-friendly **Skills graphics**, which explain the skills in simple terms, and **Skills deskmats**, which function as a reminder of the different skills.

In addition to this skill-specific instruction, **Complete Comprehension** prioritises vocabulary expansion, specifically the pre-teaching of vocabulary, as another prerequisite for successful comprehension. Every teaching unit includes a **Language toolkit**, which contains a set of **Key vocabulary** words from the comprehension text and accompanying activities to boost understanding in advance of reading.

The features outlined above are integrated into each **Complete Comprehension** teaching unit alongside enjoyable activities and discussion opportunities. These have a dual function: first, they promote reading for pleasure; second, they support pupils to engage with the text's features and build their background knowledge by exploring the themes in each text. Children are also encouraged to make comparisons with other texts and to reflect on their personal reactions to the text as readers. See pages 6 to 11 for a complete guide to the teaching unit.

The 18 teaching units in this book are designed to be completed at regular intervals over the course of a year: it is recommended that you work through six units a term. This reflects the larger proportion of time spent on teaching and embedding decoding skills in Year 1.

The comprehension skills

Each **Complete Comprehension** teaching unit targets one of the following skills, which are all essential for meaningful reading. In particular, word meaning, retrieval and inference are seen as cornerstones of comprehension, as children must be confident in these areas before they can master the remaining skills.

Key Stage 1 Comprehension skills

Word meaning 	Understand the meaning of vocabulary in the text. This symbol is used to represent word meaning in the teaching units. ▸ Go to page 14 to read more about word meaning. ▸ Word meaning is the target skill in Units 4, 6, 11, 15 and 18.
Retrieval 	Recall key details from the text. This symbol is used to represent retrieval in the teaching units. ▸ Go to page 16 to read more about retrieval. ▸ Retrieval is the target skill in Units 2, 3, 8 and 16.
Sequencing 	Put the main events in the text in order.  This symbol is used to represent sequencing in the teaching units. ▸ Go to page 18 to read more about sequencing. ▸ Sequencing is the target skill in Units 9 and 14.
Inference 	Use details from the text and background knowledge to make judgements about aspects of the text. This symbol is used to represent inference in the teaching units. ▸ Go to page 20 to read more about inference. ▸ Inference is the target skill in Units 1, 5, 7, 10, 13 and 17.
Prediction 	Use details from the text and background knowledge to make plausible predictions based on the text. This symbol is used to represent prediction in the teaching units. ▸ Go to page 22 to read more about prediction. ▸ Prediction is the target skill in Unit 12.

Structure of the teaching unit

Every **Complete Comprehension** teaching unit contains the same four components, which are explained below.

Lesson plan

The first two pages of the teaching unit allow you to see the content of the lesson at a glance. Teaching is divided into five steps to give you the flexibility to make the lesson longer or shorter according to your needs (see **Teaching with** *Complete Comprehension*, page 8). Taught as a whole, each unit provides the ideal balance of a holistic reading experience and discrete practice of reading skills.

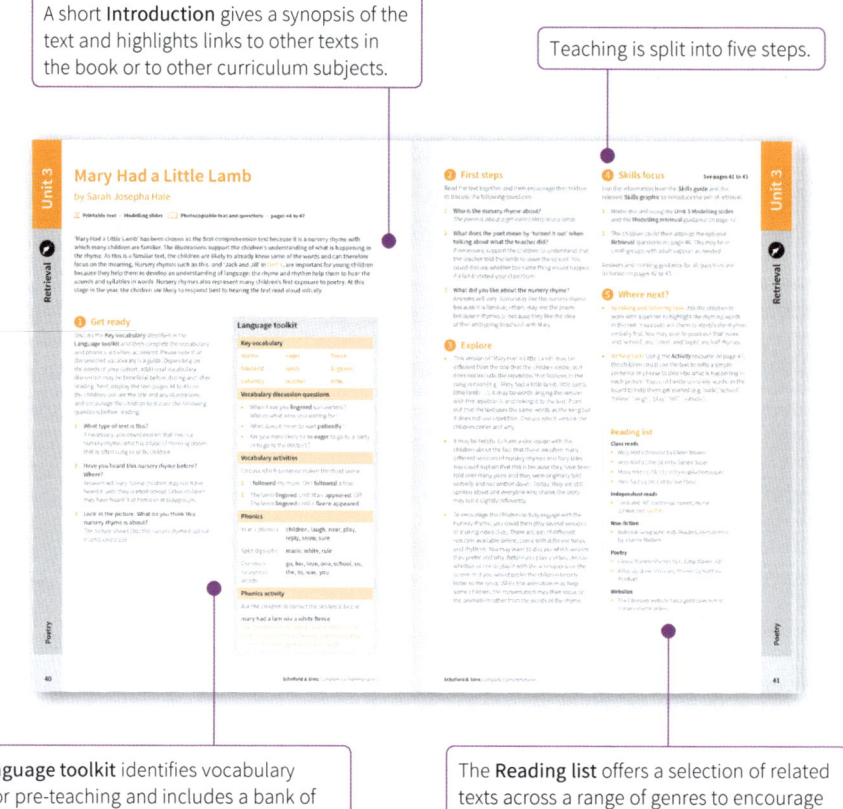

A short **Introduction** gives a synopsis of the text and highlights links to other texts in the book or to other curriculum subjects.

Teaching is split into five steps.

The **Language toolkit** identifies vocabulary terms for pre-teaching and includes a bank of supporting activities. A selection of phonics focuses are also flagged for optional discussion.

The **Reading list** offers a selection of related texts across a range of genres to encourage comparison and the strengthening of background knowledge.

Skills focus

These pages support you to model the target skill for your class using the **Let's try…** questions, which are also included in the downloadable **Modelling slides** for easy display. The mark schemes for the optional **Pupil questions**, which the children can attempt after the modelling session, are also found here.

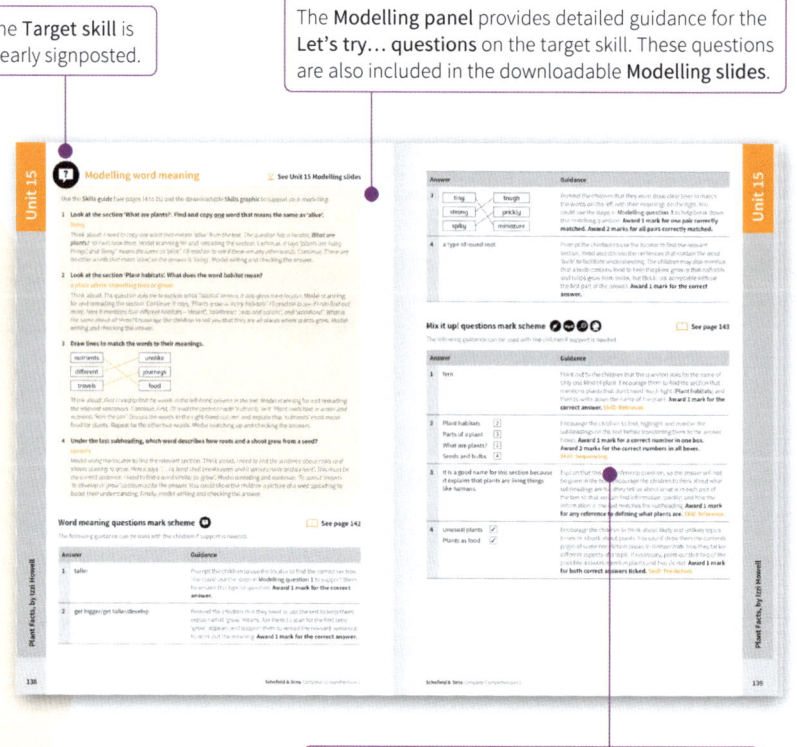

The **Target skill** is clearly signposted.

The **Modelling panel** provides detailed guidance for the Let's try… questions on the target skill. These questions are also included in the downloadable **Modelling slides**.

Mark schemes are provided for all pupil questions, and offer guidance on common areas of difficulty.

Comprehension text

The text for each unit is designed to be photocopied, or downloaded and printed, and distributed to each pupil. The lines are widely spaced to allow the children to make their own highlights and annotations. In Year 1, most children will benefit from having the text read aloud to them first.

A short, child-friendly **Introduction** helps pupils to access the text. This should be read aloud to pupils before reading the text.

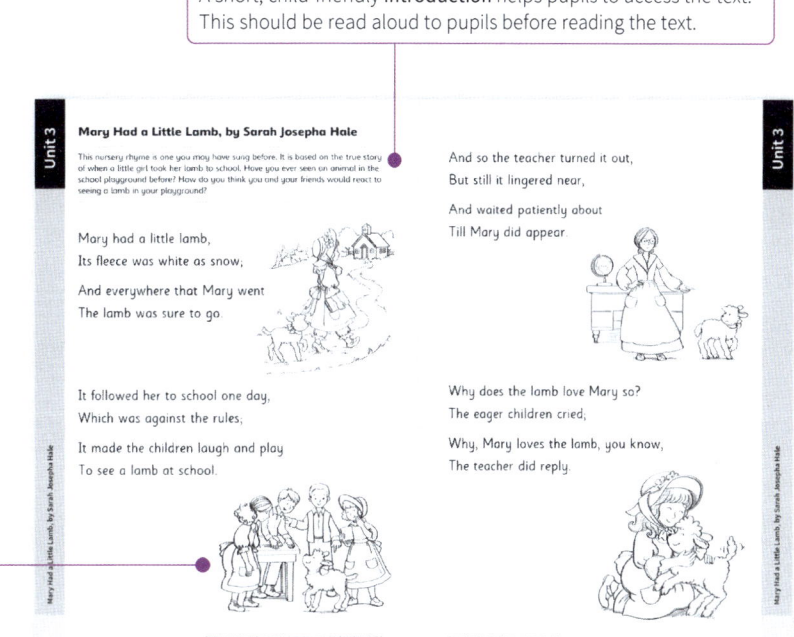

Each text includes at least one **illustration**, which should also be discussed before reading the text.

Pupil resources

Each unit ends with a set of four target-skill questions to enable the children to practise applying the target skill. The resources can be photocopied for each child.

In Units 1 to 14 of this book, there is also an additional **Activity** resource, designed to be used at the end of the teaching unit (see **Where next?**, page 11). From Unit 15 onwards, this is replaced by an additional set of **Mix it up! questions** that offer practice in a range of comprehension skills. (Please note that these are not recommended for use before the third term of Year 1.)

In *Complete Comprehension 1*, the use of all pupil resources is optional: you may choose to use them for some units and skip them for others, depending on how much time you have at your disposal, and the interests and needs of your cohort. Most Year 1 children will benefit from working in small groups with adult supervision to complete the resources.

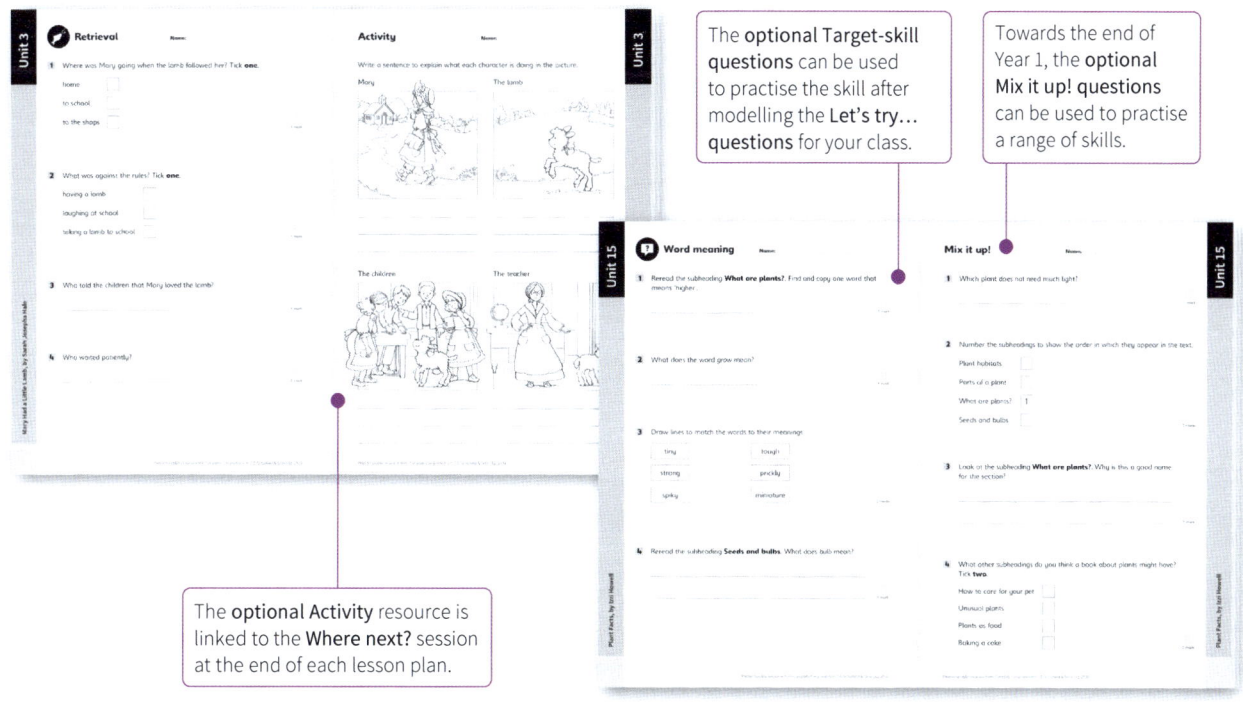

The optional **Target-skill questions** can be used to practise the skill after modelling the **Let's try… questions** for your class.

Towards the end of Year 1, the optional **Mix it up! questions** can be used to practise a range of skills.

The optional **Activity** resource is linked to the **Where next?** session at the end of each lesson plan.

Schofield & Sims Complete Comprehension 1

7

Teaching with Complete Comprehension

There are 18 teaching units in this book. They can be used flexibly, but it is recommended that they are taught consecutively, as they have been arranged in a specific order to promote discussion and build progression. There are six units to complete each term, leaving the remaining weeks free to spend on other reading work. The teaching units are followed by three optional **Progress checks** (see **Assessment**, page 11).

Each teaching unit is divided into five steps, which are shown in the diagram below. These could be taught as separate sessions over the course of a week; alternatively, multiple steps could easily be combined into a single session.

The **Get ready, First steps** and **Skills focus** steps form the backbone of each teaching unit and should be completed in order. The optional **Explore** and **Where next?** steps are intended to be adapted as necessary to fit the time you have available and the needs of your cohort.

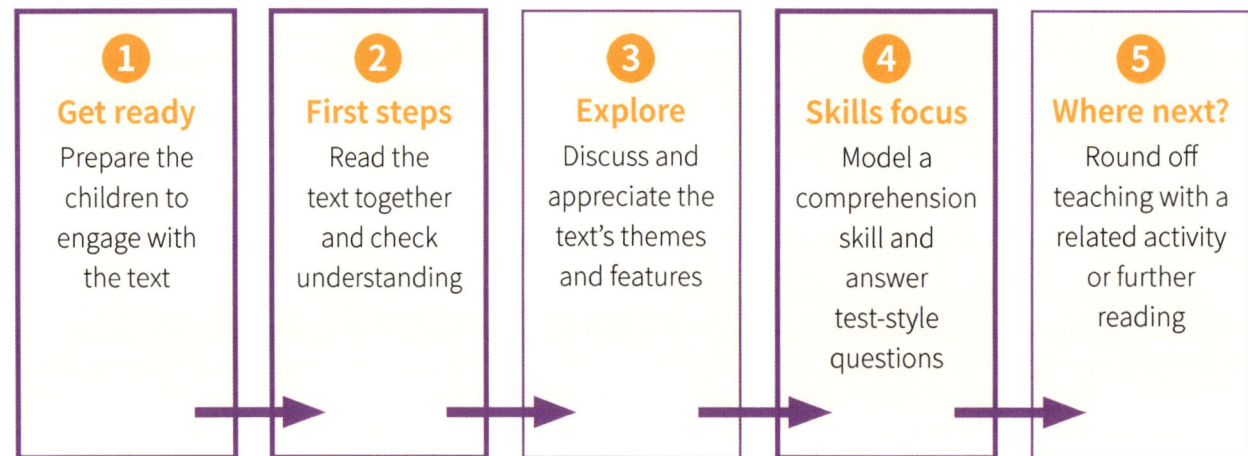

1 Get ready

The **Get ready** session is designed to be carried out verbally as a class.

Start by introducing pupils to the **Key vocabulary** terms in the **Language toolkit**. These are words from the text passage that are unusual or that the children may find difficult to read or understand. Use the **Vocabulary discussion questions** to encourage the children to use the words in context, referring to related or opposite words if desired. You could then use the **Vocabulary activities** to reinforce understanding.

At Key Stage 1, the **Phonics** section of the toolkit also includes a summary of relevant phonics covered in the text passage (e.g. split digraphs; common exception words), providing you with flexible opportunities to discuss recent learning in context. The **Phonics activity** could be used as an enjoyable class challenge to encourage the children to apply their phonics knowledge.

Once your pupils are comfortable with the language in the toolkit, display the comprehension text and accompanying illustration(s) and use the **Get ready questions** to encourage the children to access their existing knowledge of the genre and subject matter. This will ensure that their minds are fully engaged when you come to read the comprehension text together.

In the **Get ready** session, the children will:

- discuss word meanings, linking new meanings to those already known
- draw on what they already know or on background information provided by the teacher
- link what they have read or heard to their own experiences.

② First steps

Like the **Get ready** session, the **First steps** session is intended to be conducted verbally as a class.

Begin by reading the comprehension text with your class. In Year 1, the children will benefit from hearing the text read aloud initially, especially in the first two terms. The **First steps questions**, which should be discussed after reading the text, follow the order of the text and help you to ensure that the children have grasped the basic outline of the passage. The work done in this part of the teaching unit will prepare them to answer more complex questions in the **Skills focus** session (see page 10).

In the **First steps** session, the children will:

- listen to and discuss a wide range of poems, stories and non-fiction
- check that the text makes sense to them as they read, and correct inaccurate reading.

③ Explore

This optional session can be adapted to the needs of your cohort. It offers opportunities for further discussion and enrichment activities to bring the text to life.

The **Explore** discussion questions highlight key themes or literary features of the text. They support the development of analytical skills and encourage the children to express their opinions and listen to the views of their peers, promoting a culture of active reading.

The **Explore** enrichment activities might include inventing actions to go with a comic poem or using imperative verbs to instruct a partner after reading a recipe text. These activities, which represent an enjoyable change of pace within the lesson, will help to build positive attitudes to reading.

In the **Explore** session, the children will:

- learn to appreciate and recite rhymes and poems
- become very familiar with key stories, fairy stories and traditional tales, retelling them and considering their particular characteristics
- participate in discussion of what is read to them, taking turns and listening to what others say.

4 Skills focus

This is the skills-based session of the teaching unit. From Year 2 onwards, the teaching unit is always structured around three sets of questions: modelled target-skill questions (the **Let's try… questions**), practice target-skill questions and mixed skill questions. In Year 1, a simplified session is used until the middle of the third term, when the full session is introduced in Unit 15.

1 Model the target skill

First, introduce or recap the target skill, perhaps using one of the downloadable **Skills graphics** to focus the children's attention. The strategies suggested in the relevant pages of the **Skills guide** (see pages 14 to 23) may also be helpful at this point.

Once you have explained the skill, display the **Let's try… questions** (also available as a downloadable resource). Using the answers and modelling guidance provided on the **Skills focus** pages of each unit (see page 6), model the questions for your class. The modelling process is intended to be an interactive experience for the children. The **Modelling panel** contains prompts to help you keep them engaged and highlight the steps in your method.

2 Practise the target skill

In Year 1, once the **Let's try… questions** have been discussed and completed, you could choose to bring the session to a close, depending on the ability and stamina of your cohort. Alternatively, the children could increase their familiarity with the target skill by working through a set of optional **Target-skill questions**. It is recommended that Year 1 children work in small groups to complete these questions, with adult supervision as required. Answers and guidance can be found on the **Skills focus** pages of each teaching unit.

3 Practise a range of comprehension skills

From Unit 15 onwards, the session ends with a set of optional **Mix it up! questions**, which offer practice in a range of the Key Stage 1 comprehension skills. These questions are a good way to build the children's confidence in recognising questions from different skill areas. They would also work well as a homework task, if desired. Please note that these questions are not intended to be used before the third term of Year 1.

> In the **Skills focus** session, the children will:
> - discuss the significance of the title and events
> - make inferences on the basis of what is said and done
> - predict what might happen on the basis of what has been read so far
> - explain clearly their understanding of what is read to them.

5 Where next?

This optional session includes two useful resources that encourage further engagement with the text. The **Reading list** offers a selection of related texts, categorised by genre, which could be used alongside the main unit text to build background knowledge or provide some interesting contrasts. (See **The comprehension texts**, page 12, for guidance on making contrasts between the texts within this book.)

The **Speaking and listening task** and the **Writing task** can be used to help you round off the unit. In Year 1, the **Activity** resource is always linked to one of these tasks. Both tasks are closely linked to the themes in the comprehension text, and act as a bridge to other areas of the English curriculum. They also represent an opportunity for children to apply and strengthen the background knowledge they have gained in the course of the teaching unit.

> In the **Where next?** session, the children will:
> - listen to and discuss a wide range of poems, stories and non-fiction
> - develop pleasure in reading and motivation to read.

Assessment

Each **Complete Comprehension** book contains three **Progress checks**. These are informal assessments, in which the children work more independently (without the support of the full teaching unit structure) to answer a set of questions that cover a range of comprehension skills. The Progress checks can be used to boost the children's confidence and provide introductory practice for the reading component of the national tests (SATs). They are designed to be used as a helpful transition towards more formal assessment resources. Full marking guidance is provided for each question.

In Year 1, the Progress checks are intended to be completed at the end of the year, once the children are familiar with the full teaching sequence, including the **Mix it up questions** (see page 7). (From Year 2 onwards, you could choose to run a Progress check at the end of each term.) As their reading skills will still be developing, Year 1 children are likely to require extra adult help to read the texts, and may need support to write their answers to the questions.

Running the Progress checks

1. Give each child a copy of the comprehension text and spend a few minutes looking at it together, discussing the title and any illustrations. Read the pupil introduction aloud and discuss any questions the children have. In Year 1, it is a good idea to read the whole text aloud to the children at least once. You could also consider dividing the text into shorter sections if some children require further scaffolding.

2. Once all the children have read the text, you could briefly remind them of the different comprehension skills they have worked on and discuss how they can identify the questions in each skill area. You may wish to use the downloadable **Skills graphics** or refer to the **Skills guide** (see pages 14 to 23) to help with this. You could also clarify some of the vocabulary that the children have found tricky during reading, but this discussion should be brief.

3. Encourage the children to reread the text before answering the questions independently. There should be no set time allotted to this activity; allow the children to spend as long as they wish on the Progress check and encourage them to review their answers when they have finished. If they find a question challenging, support them to identify the target comprehension skill and provide them with the relevant **Skills graphic** to remind them what they need to consider when thinking about their answer.

Please note that the Progress check is a tool designed to give a brief snapshot of pupils' comprehension. It should not be used as a formal assessment but can give you an indication of areas your class are finding more challenging, which you can then use to guide your teaching.

Introduction

The comprehension texts

This book contains 21 text passages in total. The texts are arranged in themed pairs, linked by either author or subject matter. These pairings have been planned to facilitate discussion and comparison of related texts as you move through the book. They can be used alongside the external resources in each unit's **Reading list** (see page 10).

In addition to discussing the units in their intended pairs, there are many other links you can make between the texts in each book, including discussing texts of the same genre. As many of the links are cross-curricular, these extra class discussions can be a useful way to strengthen the children's background knowledge. The **Curriculum links chart** below uses shading to show the text pairs and the cross-curricular links for the texts in this book.

Curriculum links in *Complete Comprehension 1*

Unit	Title	Author	Genre	Curriculum links
1	Starting School	Jo Gray	Picture	PSHE: Describing feelings
2	Our Senses	Jo Gray	Picture	Science: Animals, including humans
3	Mary Had a Little Lamb	Sarah Josepha Hale	Poetry *Rhyme* *Traditional tale*	
4	Jack and Jill	Traditional	Poetry *Rhyme* *Traditional tale*	History: Life in different periods
5	Snow Bear	Tony Mitton	Fiction *Rhyme*	Science: Seasonal changes
6	Can't You Sleep, Little Bear?	Martin Waddell	Fiction	PSHE: Relationships, Describing feelings
7	Little Red	Jo Gray	Fiction *Traditional tale*	
8	Wolves	James Maclaine	Non-fiction *Information text*	Science: Animals, including humans
9	The Three Little Pigs	Jo Gray	Fiction *Traditional tale*	Science: Materials
10	The Three Little Pigs (Revolting Rhymes)	Roald Dahl	Poetry *Rhyme* *Traditional tale*	

Unit	Title	Author	Genre	Curriculum links
11	Looking After Rabbits	Fiona Patchett	Non-fiction *Information text*	Science: Animals, including humans
12	The Pet	Tony Bradman	Poetry *Rhyme*	
13	Chocolate Cake	Michael Rosen	Poetry	
14	Chocolate Cake Recipe	Jo Gray	Non-fiction *Instructional text*	Maths: Measurement
15	Plant Facts	Izzi Howell	Non-fiction *Information text*	Science: Plants
16	Jack and the Beanstalk	Jo Gray	Fiction *Traditional tale*	Science: Plants
17	My Two Grannies	Floella Benjamin	Fiction	Geography: Beaches PSHE: Relationships
18	Grandad Mandela	Zazi, Ziwelene and Zindzi Mandela	Non-fiction	History: Significant individuals PSHE: Relationships
Progress check 1	Bee Frog	Martin Waddell	Fiction	PSHE: Relationships; Describing feelings (Linked text: Unit 6)
Progress check 2	You Can't Take an Elephant on the Bus	Patricia Cleveland-Peck	Fiction *Rhyme*	(Linked text: Unit 12)
Progress check 3	Seaside Towns	Claire Hibbert	Non-fiction *Information text*	Geography: Beaches (Linked text: Unit 17)

Word meaning

See Units 4, 6, 11, 15 and 18

Understanding word meaning

Without an understanding of words, effective reading is impossible. As Lemov (2016)[1] remarked, 'Successful reading relies on a reader's capacity to understand both a large number of words as well as the subtleties and nuances of those words, even when words change their meaning according to the setting.' Learning to define words in context is an important skill, and one that confident readers use regularly.

It is crucial that children do not simply learn to 'define' individual words, like a dictionary, but that they understand the vocabulary they encounter in the context in which it appears. The National Curriculum (2014) requires children in Key Stage 1 to understand texts by 'drawing on what they already know or on background information or vocabulary provided by the teacher', while children in Key Stage 2 must check that a text makes sense to them by 'explaining the meaning of words in context'. Developing this skill helps children to make links between known and unknown words and teaches them to use the context of a word to interpret its meaning.

Word meaning in *Complete Comprehension*

The teaching of vocabulary can be divided into two key types: explicit and implicit instruction.[2]

Explicit instruction is the teaching of specific words and phrases that are necessary to either comprehend a specific text or comprehend meaning more generally *in advance of reading*.

Implicit instruction is the teaching of strategies that help learners assess their understanding of words *as they read*.

Word meaning is the target skill of several teaching units in each **Complete Comprehension** book. In addition, both types of vocabulary instruction are addressed in every teaching unit: explicit instruction is the focus of the **Get ready** session, in which **Key vocabulary** terms are taught before reading the comprehension passage. Implicit instruction underlies the work done in the subsequent **Explore** and **Skills focus** sessions (see pages 8 to 11 for a full description of the teaching sequence).

Word meaning questions usually require children to make links between synonyms. In **Complete Comprehension**, questions may be worded as follows:

- Which word is closest in meaning to …? Tick **one**.
- Explain what the word(s) … tell(s) you about….
- What does the word … mean in this sentence/line?
- Underline the word which tells you that….
- Draw lines to match each word to its meaning.
- Find and copy **one** word/a group of words that means the same as….

Often, questions that assess the skill of word meaning only require the child to find out one piece of information. However, this information does not usually come directly from the text but must be deduced using vocabulary knowledge. Word meaning questions thus sometimes require the use of other comprehension skills, such as inference (see page 20) to reach the correct answer.

Key challenges

As they read, many children skip over words they do not understand, losing meaning in the process. Teaching children to note down and ask about any vocabulary they do not understand when reading is therefore crucial.

Many children have relatively shallow vocabulary knowledge, only understanding a word when it appears in a familiar context. For example, many will have no trouble with 'It was *raining*' but will struggle with 'The money was *raining down*'. It is important to provide opportunities for children to deepen their knowledge by investigating words in a range of contexts.

Children with less secure vocabularies may also struggle to generate linked vocabulary (e.g. knowing that 'repeat', 'redo' and 'recycle' are all connected by the prefix 're–', which refers to doing something again). Incorporating the etymology and categorisation strategies described on page 15 when you are teaching will support the children to make these connections.

Strategies for developing word meaning

- **Context clues:** Reading around the target word or sentence to gain a general idea of the context can help children make an educated guess about the word's meaning. However, it is important to note that using context clues can also lead to confusion, as authors generally do not write with the primary aim of supporting readers to make meaning. When you use this strategy, the children should only be directed to words with a helpful context. When teaching vocabulary explicitly, it is a good idea to introduce a new word within multiple contexts before modelling how to use the specific context to construct meaning. The vocabulary discussion questions in each unit's **Language toolkit** (see page 6) help the children to understand the **Key vocabulary** terms in context.

- **Substitution:** Encourage the children to make substitutions to help them check the meaning of a word. If the target word is replaced by a new word, does the sentence still make sense? Is the new word a synonym, or has the meaning of the sentence changed? If the sentence still 'works', how does this information help the children to answer the question?

- **Shades of meaning:** When the children are investigating possible synonyms for unfamiliar vocabulary, ensure that they understand that a synonym is similar to, but not the same as, the original word. Asking the children to place a group of synonyms on a scale from the weakest to the strongest can help them to appreciate nuances.

- **Categorisation:** For vocabulary knowledge to become deeper and more securely embedded, the children need to be able to categorise vocabulary. For example, knowing that 'zebra' and 'mongoose' both refer to animals, and that 'angry' and 'exasperated' both describe negative feelings, will support the children to make essential links as they read. Providing them with word cards to sort into categories can help to build up this understanding.

- **Etymology:** Children need to be taught the meanings of root words, prefixes and suffixes, and should be encouraged to use these to help them make educated guesses about word meaning. Throughout **Complete Comprehension**, and especially at Key Stage 2, etymology activities are included in the **Vocabulary activities** section of the **Language toolkit**.

Modelling word meaning

When modelling word meaning for your class using the **Let's try… questions** (see page 6), the steps below may be useful. Specific modelling guidance is also provided in the relevant teaching units.

1. Read aloud. Model reading the whole question carefully.
2. Identify and underline the key words in the question.
3. Model scanning the text efficiently to locate each key word, or related key words, from the question.
4. Demonstrate reading the sentences before and after each key word to look for context clues.
5. Make links aloud between the key words and their synonyms. Model using this knowledge to help you gauge the meaning.
6. Formulate an answer. Model checking that it answers the question.

---

1 Lemov, D. (2016) *Reading Reconsidered*. San Francisco: Jossey Bass, p. 251.
2 Lemov (2016), pp. 253–256.

Retrieval

See Units 2, 3, 8 and 16

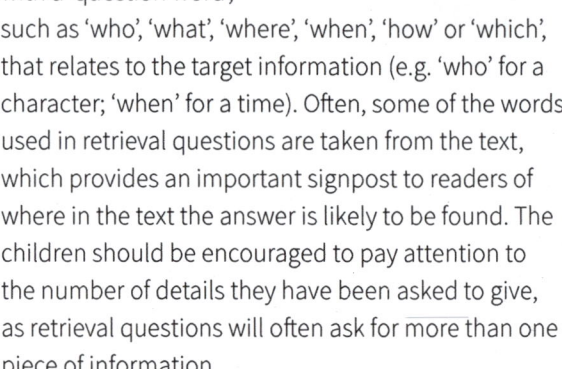

Understanding retrieval

Retrieval is the act of efficiently locating, and reproducing, important details in a text. Other reading skills cannot be mastered without a knowledge of retrieval, which is often seen as the most important reading skill.

The National Curriculum (2014) requires children in Key Stage 1 to 'identify/explain key aspects of fiction and non-fiction texts', while children in Key Stage 2 must 'retrieve and record information/identify key details from fiction and non-fiction'. Strong retrieval skills are essential for effective comprehension.

Retrieval in *Complete Comprehension*

Retrieval relies on a secure understanding of the information in a text. The key to successful retrieval is remembering that the information required to answer the question is always stated explicitly in the text. The children must be encouraged to focus on the text rather than relying on memory or on their extrinsic knowledge (in contrast to other comprehension skills, such as inference – see page 20).

Because it is so important, retrieval is the focus skill in many of the units in each **Complete Comprehension** book. This allows the children to practise retrieval in many different contexts. In addition, further retrieval practice is built into every teaching unit through the questions in the **First steps** session (see page 9) of the lesson. These straightforward questions encourage the children to develop the habit of looking back at the text after their initial reading to pick out key details. This helps them to generate a 'mental model' of the text, which will give them a better idea of where to look for answers when they encounter more formal questions in the **Skills focus** session (see page 6).

In **Complete Comprehension**, retrieval questions often begin with a 'question word', such as 'who', 'what', 'where', 'when', 'how' or 'which', that relates to the target information (e.g. 'who' for a character; 'when' for a time). Often, some of the words used in retrieval questions are taken from the text, which provides an important signpost to readers of where in the text the answer is likely to be found. The children should be encouraged to pay attention to the number of details they have been asked to give, as retrieval questions will often ask for more than one piece of information.

In **Complete Comprehension**, retrieval questions are often worded as follows:

- Who…/What…/When…/ Where…/How…/ Which…?
- Give **two**…
- According to the text…
- Find and copy **two** examples of … from the text.
- Draw lines to match each statement…
- Tick to show whether the statement is true or false.
- Tick to show whether the statement(s) below is/are fact or opinion.

It is important to note that retrieval questions will sometimes require the children to draw on other comprehension skills, such as inference (see page 20), to reach the correct answer.

Key challenges

Some children find retrieval difficult; they try to remember the information or use their extrinsic knowledge to answer questions, instead of referring back to the text. When teaching retrieval, you must emphasise the fact that the information will always be found in the text.

Strategies for developing retrieval

- **Identify key words:** To retrieve information, the children need to be able to identify key words in the question before locating them in the text. This should be modelled explicitly by looking at the question, removing any extraneous information, and then deciding on the key words needed. Sometimes, the key words in the question will be synonymous with words in the text. It is important to model discussing possible synonyms that the text may use instead of the key words.

- **Scanning:** Scanning is the process of rapidly searching the text for specific information, such as a key word. This is a fundamental reading skill that should be prioritised and practised. It is important to model a systematic approach by scanning every line of the text, perhaps using your finger or a ruler on the page. Activities that do not require the children to decode may be helpful for developing scanning skills. The children could use 'search and find' texts, such as the *Where's Wally?* books, to practise scanning. Alternatively, you could provide a section of text and challenge the children to see how many words, letter strings or punctuation marks they can find in it within a given time.

- **Point out the evidence/Fastest finger first:** To emphasise the importance of always referring to the text rather than falling back on extrinsic knowledge, challenge the children to 'point out the evidence' for their answer, for example by highlighting, circling or underlining the text. You could also play games such as 'Fastest finger first', in which players race to physically place their finger on the word(s) in the text that answer a question or provide a relevant detail.

Modelling retrieval

When modelling retrieval for your class using the **Let's try… questions** (see page 6), the steps below may be useful. Specific modelling guidance is also provided in the relevant teaching units.

1. Read the question aloud. Remind the children that they should resist the temptation to draw conclusions based on their own knowledge, and model focusing your attention back to the words in the text.

2. Locate the key words in your concept or question.

3. Scan the text for those key words, or related key words, and highlight or underline them.

4. If necessary, read around the key words to look for context clues.

5. Find the information you need in the text and highlight or underline it.

6. Check that the information you have found answers the question.

Sequencing

See Units 9 and 14

Understanding sequencing

Sequencing is the act of ordering the events or information in a text. Although this may sound straightforward, sequencing is a complex skill that relies on a secure understanding of the whole text. Children must be able to retrieve key details from the text and then use this information to work out the chronology of events, alternating between focusing on sections of the text and the text as a whole. Sequencing is important for reading longer texts and for understanding the whole of a text. The National Curriculum (2014) requires children in Key Stage 1 to discuss 'the sequence of events in books and how items of information are related'. Almost every other reading skill requires the ability to sequence and retell the events and information in a text. As with the skill of retrieval (see page 16), the key to successful sequencing is to use evidence from the whole text, rather than relying on memory.

Sequencing in *Complete Comprehension*

Sequencing is the focus skill for a number of units in the **Complete Comprehension** books aimed at children in Key Stage 1. Additional sequencing practice is also built into every unit through the **First steps** session (see page 9). The **First steps** questions, which encourage children to recall the most important points from the text, are in chronological order: this helps the children to generate a 'mental model' of the text and develop a better idea of the sequence of events in the text as a whole.

In **Complete Comprehension**, the skill of sequencing is often assessed using a 'sequencing statements' format, in which children are asked to write numbers in boxes next to a list of four or five sentences to show the order in which events from the text happened, as in the example below:

Number the events to show the order in which they happened in the story.

The wolf tried to get the three little pigs.	2
The pigs built their own houses.	1
The pigs lived happily ever after.	4
The wolf ran away.	3

Sequencing questions also often begin with a 'question word', such as 'who', 'what', 'when' or 'which', that relates to the target information (e.g. 'who' for a character, 'when' for a time). Often, some of the words used in sequencing questions are taken from the text, which provides an important signpost to readers of where in the text the answer is likely to be found. In **Complete Comprehension**, sequencing questions may be worded as follows:

- Think about the whole story…
- Sort these…
- Which of these events happened first? Tick **one**.
- What did … do first/before/after/as soon as … ?
- When in the story did…?
- Look at the first/second/third paragraph. Which event happened first/last? Tick **one**.

Key challenges

Sequencing requires a secure understanding of the text and a good working memory. Children sometimes struggle to sequence information from a text because they cannot keep track of all of its constituent parts. This is because sequencing carries a high cognitive load – readers have to decode and retrieve information, then rely on their working memory to order that information. They must then use their knowledge of time adverbs and conjunctions to understand what they are being asked to do and respond appropriately to the sequencing activity.

Strategies for developing sequencing

- **Simplified sequencing:** You could reduce the cognitive load of sequencing by using images to represent events in a text, or by reducing the number of statements that the children need to sequence.

- **Sequencing vocabulary:** To answer sequencing questions, the children need to understand the relevant vocabulary. It is important to discuss and draw attention to sequencing language such as 'first', 'after', 'next', 'finally' and 'once upon a time' as you read, both in English lessons and across the curriculum.

- **Physical sequencing:** Sometimes children struggle to sequence large chunks of text. If this is the case, separate the text into sections and then cut those sections up, modelling your thinking process as you physically order and sequence the parts of the text. This is especially useful when modelling how to answer a 'sequencing statements' question.

- **Skim-reading:** Skim-reading means reading a text quickly to assimilate the main ideas. It enables children to gain an overview of what each section of a text is about. This helps them to create a mental map of the text and to predict where information is most likely to be found. This strategy is particularly helpful when reading non-fiction. You could introduce skim-reading by showing the children the text with most lines blacked out, so that only the title and first sentence of each paragraph are visible. Discuss what this content tells the reader about the paragraph or section. Encourage the children to use the first line of a paragraph to 'get the gist' of the text before reading it in more detail. It is also worth reminding them to look at titles, subheadings, illustrations, captions and any words that are formatted in bold or italics.

- **Graphic organisers:** The children may benefit from using a graphic organiser to support their sequencing of a text. It is important to explicitly model your thought process as you demonstrate these strategies. Examples of useful graphic organisers include:

    - Story maps: The children map out the main events in a text by drawing pictures that represent the key points and linking these using arrows.
    - Storyboards: The children draw six key events from the story and write captions for them.
    - Timelines: The children put the key events of the story into chronological order.
    - Beginning, middle, end: The children draw or write the main event for the beginning, middle and end of the text.
    - Story mountains: The children write the key events of the story using the following headings to structure their ideas: 'beginning', 'build-up', 'problem', 'resolution' and 'ending'.

Modelling sequencing

When modelling sequencing for your class using the **Let's try… questions** (see page 6), the steps below may be useful. Specific modelling guidance can also be found in the relevant teaching units.

1. Read the question aloud. Tell the children they must use the text when they sequence, rather than relying on their memory.

2. Locate the information you need to sequence. Model identifying whether you are sequencing multiple points or one point.

3. Skim-read the text to locate the relevant point(s) for sequencing. Highlight or underline each point.

4. Model ordering the information.

5. Check that the information you have ordered answers the question.

Inference

See Units 1, 5, 7, 10, 13 and 17

Understanding inference

Inference skills are essential for understanding our world: we use them whenever we gauge other people's emotions using their facial expressions or tone of voice. Children will therefore have some ability to infer even before they learn to decode.

Inference is often described as the ability to 'read between the lines' or 'find clues' in a text. However, it can be more helpfully defined as the skill of using both evidence from the text and our background knowledge to come to a reasonable conclusion.

Academics have separated inference-making into a number of distinct categories (Kispal, 2008).[3] However, most recognise two main categories of inference:

Coherence inferences are necessary for basic comprehension. They can be formulated from understanding a text's cohesive devices, such as pronouns, or from linking background knowledge to the text. For example, from the sentence 'Maggie loved playing catch but sometimes she refused to bring the ball back', we could infer that 'Maggie', 'she' and 'her' are the same (using cohesive devices), and that Maggie is probably a dog (using background knowledge).

Elaborative inferences are not necessary for basic comprehension, but they make a text more interesting. An elaborative inference might be a prediction or speculation that the reader makes about a character or the consequences of an action. For example, from the sentence 'Maggie loved playing catch but sometimes she refused to give the ball back to her owner', we could infer that, because she sometimes refused to bring back the ball, Maggie might be a puppy. Elaborative inferences depend on background knowledge and are thus more demanding than coherence inferences.

The National Curriculum (2014) requires pupils in Key Stage 1 to be 'making inferences on the basis of what is being said and done'. At Key Stage 2, learners must rely on their background knowledge, 'drawing inferences such as inferring characters' feelings, thoughts and motives'.

Inference in *Complete Comprehension*

Inference is the focus skill in a high proportion of the units in each **Complete Comprehension** book, to allow the children to practise inference in different contexts.

In **Complete Comprehension**, inference questions often include the phrase 'How/Why do you think…'. It is a good idea to draw the children's attention to this wording to help them remember that they need to make a judgement using their own knowledge *in addition to* the text, rather than limiting themselves to details explicitly mentioned in the text, as they would when answering a retrieval (see page 16) or sequencing (see page 18) question. Once the children's inference skills have begun to embed, some questions will require them to provide evidence to support their inferences. You should explore the expectations of these questions with the children.

In **Complete Comprehension**, inference questions are often worded as follows:

- Why…/How…/Which…?
- Why/How/What do you think…? Explain your answer.
- How can you tell…?
- Explain why…
- Give two reasons…
- True or false…
- Think about the whole text. What impression do you get of …? Give **one** impression and **one** piece of evidence.

It is important to note that inference questions always require the use of other comprehension skills, such as retrieval (see page 16), to reach the correct answer.

Key challenges

For many children, inference is a real challenge. This is because they are required to make an intuitive leap to move from what they *know* (direct evidence that they can see in the text) to what they *think* (the conclusion they come to after locating and assessing the evidence). An understanding of the text, robust vocabulary skills and strong background knowledge are essential prerequisites for successful inference-making. The skills of word meaning (see page 14) and retrieval (see page 16) must therefore be embedded before inference skills can fully develop.

Strategies for developing inference

- **Think-alouds:** Confident readers make inferences automatically as they read. However, when teaching children to infer, you should slow down and model your thought process. 'Think-alouds' (statements that verbalise your thought process) can be useful. For example, you could think aloud to model dividing your thoughts into two types: 'what I know' and 'what I think' (e.g. 'From the text, I know that… This makes me think…'). Think-alouds can also be used to model refining an inference (e.g. 'I thought that… because… but… so…'), and can be incorporated into the strategies below.

- **Inference check:** Marzano (2010)[4] suggested that teachers could support inference-making by modelling asking the following four questions:

    1. 'What is my inference?'
    2. 'What did I use to make my inference?'
    3. 'How good was my thinking?'
    4. 'Do I need to change my thinking?'

    These questions could be used in the strategy above.

- **Objects and visual representations:** Using objects and images that relate to the text can be helpful when exploring inference, as this eliminates the need to decode and therefore reduces cognitive load. You could use images to represent characters or scenes from the text, and model inference by adding thought or speech bubbles to them. Alternatively, you could assign objects to characters from a text. For example, if you were reading 'The Three Bears', you could provide different porridge bowls and ask the children to decide which character each bowl is most likely to belong to.

- **Real-life scenarios:** Many children will need prompting to connect the inferences they make in everyday life with inferences made while reading. One strategy is to use models such as 'think-alouds' to explore real-life scenarios, using clues to make inferences about people's preferences, location or relationship. For instance, you could listen to a conversation or watch a video clip showing two people and ask the children what they can infer about their relationship (e.g. 'Do you think these people are friends or enemies? How can you tell from what they do and what they say?').

- **Graphic organisers:** These are especially helpful when the children are asked to provide evidence or an explanation for their inferences. For example, the children could complete a 'I can see…I know…I think' chart: a table with three columns in which they first record what they can see in the text or image. They then record what they know from the text, and use this to write what they think (the inference). It is important to explicitly model the thinking process behind this strategy.

Modelling inference

When modelling the skill of inference for your class using the **Let's try… questions** (see page 6), the steps below may be useful. Specific modelling guidance is also provided in the teaching units.

1. Read the question aloud.
2. Locate the key words in the question. Scan the text for those key words, or related key words, and highlight or underline them.
3. Read around the key words to look for context clues.
4. Discuss what the text tells you about the key words.
5. Model using this information to make an inference. This might involve relating the ideas in the question to your own experiences to model the use of background knowledge.
6. Model justifying your inference with evidence from the text.
7. Check that the information answers the question.

---

3 Kispal, A. (2008) Effective Teaching of Inference Skills for Reading. *Literature Review*. Research Report DCSF-RR031, National Foundation for Educational Research.

4 Marzano, R.J. (2010) The Art and Science of Teaching/Teaching Inference. *Educational Leadership,* 67(7), pp.80–81.

Prediction

See Unit 12

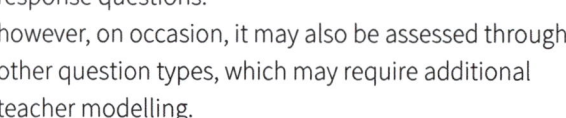

Understanding prediction

Prediction is the skill of being able to make inferences (see page 20) about what is likely to happen later in a text. In a fiction extract, this might relate to a character's actions; in a non-fiction extract, it might be about the type of information that will be found in the next part of the text. A skilled reader makes predictions automatically, finding links between known and new information as they read. The National Curriculum (2014) requires pupils in Key Stage 1 to predict 'what might happen on the basis of what has been read so far' while Key Stage 2 children need to predict 'what might happen from details stated and implied'. The ability to make predictions requires a thorough understanding of a passage. To make a plausible prediction, the reader must be able to select details from the text and use these, and their own background knowledge, to decide what is likely to happen.

The skill of prediction is usually assessed through tick-box or extended response questions: however, on occasion, it may also be assessed through other question types, which may require additional teacher modelling.

Key challenges

Often, children with poor comprehension skills will be able to formulate a prediction, but their predictions will not be sufficiently plausible, and may not be linked to the original text. You should remind all children to use the text to inform any prediction and underlying inference; this can also help when answering prediction questions that require additional justification, which can be challenging. (For more information on the challenges of teaching and using inference, see page 20.)

Prediction in *Complete Comprehension*

One teaching unit in each **Complete Comprehension** book focuses on prediction. In addition, the children's prediction skills are engaged in the **Get ready** session of every unit. These questions encourage the children to use the title and any subheadings, illustration(s) and their own background knowledge to help them predict what a passage will be about. Following on from this, the **Mix it up! questions** in the **Skills focus** session offer frequent opportunities to practise and refine this important skill. (See pages 6 to 11 for a complete guide to the teaching unit.)

As prediction requires the use of inference skills, it is not surprising that prediction questions are often worded similarly to inference questions. Once the children's prediction skills have begun to embed, they will often be asked to justify their predictions using the text. In **Complete Comprehension**, prediction questions may be worded as follows:

- Who…/What…/When…/Where…/How…/Which…?
- Predict…
- Imagine…
- Which is most likely…?

Strategies for developing prediction

- **'Think-alouds':** One way to support children to predict is to use 'think-alouds' (statements that verbalise your thought process). You can use think-alouds at different points to model prediction:
  - Before reading (e.g. 'I've found this book and when I look at the title/illustrations I think… because… so that might mean… I could predict…').
  - While reading (e.g. 'I wonder what's going to happen next. I know… So that makes me think… I could predict…').
  - After reading (e.g. 'While I was reading I predicted… I was right because/I was incorrect because…').

- **Multiple predictions:** Confident readers not only make predictions, but they also constantly re-evaluate and adjust their predictions as they read. One way to help the children develop this skill is to start from a narrow viewpoint: for example, you could show them a small part of an illustration or a phrase from the text and ask them make a prediction based on what they can see, then show them more of the picture/text and ask them to make another prediction. This will help them to adjust their first prediction as they read.

- **Making links:** Making plausible predictions involves making links to other known texts, characters and information. Although predictions should be made with reference to a specific text, extrinsic knowledge relating to the wider genre or subject matter of the text is also important. For instance, if you are reading 'Cinderella' with your class and the children have read other fairy tales, they will know that in a fairy tale the main character usually lives happily ever after, and this could have a bearing on any predictions they make. As part of the 'think-aloud' process detailed above, you could model making links to known texts and different types of text. In **Complete Comprehension**, each extract has at least one linked text; listed on pages 12 to 13 and often referred to in the each unit's introduction, these links are designed to help you make connections with the children's existing knowledge. Each unit also includes a **Reading list** of related texts.

- **Graphic organisers:** Once the children have started to make predictions, you could use graphic organisers to help them organise their ideas and scaffold their justifications. It is important to explicitly model the thinking process behind this strategy. Examples of useful graphic organisers for prediction include:

    - 'I predict… because': The children complete a chart that asks them to record their predictions and their justification.

    - 'What has happened… What will happen… What actually happened': The children complete a chart by recording event(s) from the text and their predictions about what will happen next. You could then give them copies of the source text and allow them to read beyond the extract and record what actually happened.

Modelling prediction

When modelling the skill of prediction for your class using the **Let's try… questions** (see page 6), the steps below may be useful. Specific modelling guidance is also provided in the teaching units.

1. Read the question aloud. Point out the need to look back at the text rather than making a hasty prediction that does not relate closely enough to the text – the children need to think about what is *likely* to happen rather than what they *want* to happen.

2. Locate the key words in the question. Scan the text for those key words, or related key words, and highlight or underline them.

3. Read around the key words to look for context clues.

4. Discuss what you know already.

5. Discuss what you think may happen next, linking this back to the text.

6. Model justifying your prediction. This might involve relating the ideas in the question to your own experiences to model using your background knowledge.

7. Check that the information in your answer matches the question.

Unit 1

Inference

Starting School
(Picture comprehension)

▽ **Printable text** • **Modelling slides**   📖 **Photocopiable text and questions** • **pages 28 to 31**

The first two units of this book use pictures instead of texts to help introduce the children to the structure of the teaching units and to reduce the cognitive load of encountering the comprehension skills for the first time. The picture for this unit shows a group of children in a classroom. It is ideal for introducing the skill of inference, as the children will be able to focus on relating their own experiences to the picture without the need to decode. In addition, this is an opportunity for the children to learn that, although they might feel one way about an experience, others may feel differently – some children feel excited about school and others feel nervous. It is important to emphasise that there is no right or wrong way to feel.

❶ Get ready

Discuss the **Key vocabulary** identified in the **Language toolkit** and then complete the vocabulary and phonics activities as desired. At this point in Year 1, the **Key vocabulary** words are intended to be used as a tool for discussion. As it is unlikely that the children will be able to decode these words independently, it is important that you read them aloud. Next, display the picture (page 28) and encourage the children to discuss the following questions.

1   **What can you see in this picture?**
    Answers will vary. Encourage the children to extend their answers by referring to details from the picture.

2   **Looking at the vocabulary words and the picture, what do you think we will be talking about in this unit?**
    The words are all about our feelings. I think in this unit we might talk about how children feel when they start school.

3   **What do you think we can do when trying to read the names of the children in the picture?**
    I think we will need to use phonics to sound out/ decode words.

Language toolkit

Key vocabulary

amused	angry	bored
excited	happy	helpful
nervous	upset	worried

Vocabulary discussion questions

- When would you feel **excited**?
- When are you **helpful**?
- When have you felt **bored**?

Vocabulary activities

Discuss which sentence makes the most sense.

1   I hurt my knee and felt **upset**. OR
    I hurt my knee and felt **happy**.

2   I was **amused** when you were being silly. OR
    I was **amused** when my friend was hurt.

Phonics

The children should be able to decode the names of the children in the picture.

Phonics activity

Ask the children to correct the sentence below.

the boy wos worried
The children should add a capital letter to the start and a full stop to the end. Some may also correct the spelling of 'was'.

Picture

2 First steps

Read the text together and then encourage the children to discuss the following questions.

1. **Who is in the picture?**
   Encourage the children to read the names of the different children in the picture.

2. **What is your favourite part of the picture? Why?**
   Answers will vary (e.g. *My favourite part is the girls laughing on the mat/the boy cheering at the computer, because they are having fun*).

3. **How did you feel when you started Year 1?**
   Answers will vary. Some children may have been excited; others may have felt nervous. Encourage them to explore their feelings using the **Key vocabulary** and emphasise that there is no right or wrong answer – not everyone feels the same about everything.

3 Explore

- Using the picture to help, encourage the children to think about the different feelings that they experience when they are in school. Scribe these on the board for the children to see. Spend time discussing what the emotions mean and ask the children if they can think of other words for the same feeling. Encourage them to show what each feeling looks like by using face and body gestures.

- To take this further and help the children to understand a range of feelings, you could use the **Feelings cards** on page 29 to discuss specific emotions. Encourage the children to think about how they would respond emotionally to different scenarios. Tailor the scenarios to suit your group of children. You may also want to explore the feelings of characters from books and films. See the **Reading list** for some useful resources.

4 Skills focus   See pages 26 to 27

Use the information from the **Skills guide** and the relevant **Skills graphic** to introduce the skill of inference.

1. Model the skill using the **Unit 1 Modelling slides** and the **Modelling inference** guidance on page 26.

2. The children could then attempt the optional **Inference** questions on page 30. This may be in small groups with adult support as needed.

Answers and marking guidance for all questions are included on pages 26 to 27.

5 Where next?

- **Speaking and listening task:** Play a game of 'Simon says' with the children, substituting feeling phrases for the usual actions (e.g. 'Simon says, look happy'). In between commands you could ask questions about those feelings (e.g. 'What makes you feel happy?'). Once the children have played this game a few times, split them into groups of four and encourage them to play the game together, taking it in turns to be 'Simon' and give the commands.

- **Writing task:** In small groups, or as a class, the children could use the **Activity** resource on page 31 to write words to describe how the children in the pictures are feeling. Use the word bank to help them get started. As a class, you could then write down some synonyms and antonyms for these words (e.g. sad, unhappy, surprised, etc.) to boost the children's understanding of feelings.

Reading list

Class reads
- *Come to School Too, Blue Kangaroo!* by Emma Chichester Clark
- *Harry and the Dinosaurs Go to School* by Ian Whybrow
- *The Huge Bag of Worries* by Virginia Ironside
- *I Am Too Absolutely Small for School* by Lauren Child
- *Lucy and Tom at School* by Shirley Hughes
- *Starting School* by Allan Ahlberg
- *Topsy and Tim: Start School* by Jean Adamson
- *What's Going On Inside My Head?* by Molly Potter

Independent reads
- *Going to School* by Rose Blake
- *Lots of Things to Spot at School* by Katie Daynes

Non-fiction
- *The Great Big Book of Feelings* by Mary Hoffman
- *How Are You Feeling Today?* by Molly Potter
- *Stuff to Know When You Start School* by DK Children

Poetry
- *Poems About Emotions* by Brian Moses

Films
- *Inside Out* (Disney, 2015)

Websites
- The KS1 area of the BBC Bitesize website contains a good selection of video clips about emotional wellbeing.

Modelling inference

▽ See Unit 1 Modelling slides

Use the **Skills guide** (see pages 20 to 21) and the downloadable **Skills graphic** to support your modelling.

1. **How is Tom feeling? Tick one.**

    cross ☐
    worried ☐
    scared ☐
    excited ☑

    Explain that, first of all, you need to read the question. Ask: *What is the question asking me?* and highlight the key words (Tom/feeling/Tick one). Discuss the meaning of the possible answers. You could ask the children to show you what these feelings look like using their faces. Think aloud: *Now I need to find Tom in the picture and look at his face.* Encourage the children to help you find Tom. Continue: *Tom looks happy, but 'happy' isn't one of the possible answers. Tom is putting his arms in the air so he might be feeling something stronger than happiness. What other words mean 'happy'?* Encourage the children to come up with some ideas. Continue: *'Excited' is on the list. I think Tom is excited.* Discuss why Tom might be excited. Model ticking one answer only and checking it against the question.

2. **Who is feeling happy? Tick one.**

    Jess ☑
    Wan ☐
    Nat ☐
    Max ☐

    Remind the children that first you need to read the question. Ask: *What is the question asking me?* and highlight the key words. Think aloud: *Tom and Uma look happy but their names are not on the list of possible answers. I need to look at who is on the list.* Encourage the children to help you look at the list and circle the names and/or faces of the children in the picture. Discuss words that mean 'happy'. Think aloud: *Wan looks worried, Max looks angry and Nat looks bored, so that leaves Jess. Yes, I think Jess is happy, as she is smiling at Uma.* Model ticking one answer only and checking it against the question.

3. **Which word best describes how Nat is feeling? Tick one.**

    joyful ☐
    excited ☐
    bored ☑
    silly ☐

    Ask the children to tell you what you need to do first (read the question). Ask: *What is the question asking me?* and highlight the key words. Ask: *What do we need to do next?* (find Nat in the picture). Think aloud: *Nat looks upset and uninterested but these words are not on the list of possible answers.* Encourage the children to suggest what to do next (look at the list of possible answers). Think aloud: *Nat does not look joyful, excited or silly. I think she doesn't want to do her work. I think she is bored.* Model ticking one answer only and checking it against the question.

4. **Why is Wan nervous?**

    He is nervous about going into the classroom.

    Explain that, for this question, there are no answers to tick and, instead, you need to write your own answer. Think aloud: *The key words in this question are 'why', 'Wan' and 'nervous'. I know from the question that I need to look at Wan in the picture.* Encourage the children to find Wan. Think aloud: *Wan is peering around the wall of the classroom and he hasn't come in like everybody else. If I didn't want to go somewhere, this might be how I would act.* Ask the children to discuss why Wan might be feeling nervous. Continue: *I think Wan is nervous about going into the classroom, so I need to write this in a sentence.* Model writing an answer and checking it against the question.

Inference questions mark scheme

See page 30

The following guidance can be used with the children if support is needed.

	Answer	Guidance
1	angry ✓	Remind the children to read the question and highlight the key words. Then encourage them to find Max in the picture and to look at the words in the list of possible answers. Support them to find the answer that matches Max's facial expression. Remind them to tick one answer only. **Award 1 mark for the correct answer ticked.**
2	Fizz ✓	Remind the children to read the question and highlight the key words. Then encourage them to look at the list of possible answers and circle the names and/or faces of the children in the picture. Ask them to think about words that mean 'upset' and who looks upset in the picture. Remind them to tick one answer only. **Award 1 mark for the correct answer ticked.**
3	happy ✓	Encourage the children to highlight the key words in the question and to find Jess in the picture. Then ask them to look at the list of possible answers. Remind them to tick one answer only. **Award 1 mark for the correct answer ticked.**
4	He is worried that Fizz is hurt.	Explain that the lines beneath the question mean that this question needs a written answer. Encourage the children to find Seb in the picture. Ask them to think about why Seb might be feeling worried. Encourage them to write this down and to check their answer against the question. **Award 1 mark for any reference to Fizz being injured.**

Unit 1

Starting School

How did you feel when you came to school this morning? How did you feel before your first ever day at school?

Feelings cards

Listen to your teacher. Can you point to the correct picture?

upset	happy

bored	amused

worried	angry

Unit 1

Inference

Name: _____

1 How is Max feeling? Tick **one**.

- happy ☐
- excited ☐
- worried ☐
- angry ☐

1 mark

2 Who is feeling upset? Tick **one**.

- Tom ☐
- Uma ☐
- Fizz ☐
- Jess ☐

1 mark

3 Which word best describes how Jess is feeling? Tick **one**.

- annoyed ☐
- sad ☐
- happy ☐
- concerned ☐

1 mark

4 Why is Seb worried?

_____

_____

1 mark

Photocopiable resource from *Complete Comprehension 1* © Schofield & Sims Ltd, 2020.

Starting School

Activity

Name: _____

How is each child feeling? Write a word from the word bank under each picture. One has been done for you.

happy

_____

_____

_____

_____

_____

Word bank

~~happy~~   angry   worried   upset   bored   excited

Photocopiable resource from *Complete Comprehension 1* © Schofield & Sims Ltd, 2020.

Our Senses
(Picture comprehension)

Unit 2 — Retrieval — Picture

▽ **Printable text** • **Modelling slides**   📖 **Photocopiable text and questions** • pages 36 to 39

This unit is the second of two picture comprehensions designed to introduce Year 1 children to the structure of the teaching unit and to reduce the cognitive load of encountering the comprehension skills for the first time. The picture for this unit, which shows a group of children using their senses in a range of activities, provides a helpful link to the science curriculum for this age group.

1 Get ready

Discuss the **Key vocabulary** identified in the **Language toolkit** and then complete the vocabulary and phonics activities as desired. At this point in Year 1, the **Key vocabulary** words are intended to be used as a tool for discussion. As it is unlikely that the children will be able to decode these words independently, it is important that you read them aloud. Next, display the picture (page 36) and encourage the children to discuss the following questions.

1. **What can you see in this picture?**
   Answers will vary. Encourage the children to extend their answers by referring to details from the picture.

2. **Looking at the vocabulary words and the picture, what do you think we will be talking about in this unit?**
   I think we will be talking about our senses and how we use them.

3. **What do you think we can do when trying to read the names of the children in the picture?**
   I think we will need to use phonics to sound out/decode words.

Language toolkit

Key vocabulary

feel	hear	look
see	sight	smell
sound	taste	touch

Vocabulary discussion questions

- What is your favourite **smell**?
- What **sounds** have you heard that are loud?
- What do you like to **look** at?

Vocabulary activities

Discuss which sentence makes the most sense.

1. I could **taste** a tree. *OR*
   I could **taste** chocolate.

2. I used my hand to **touch**. *OR*
   I used my hand to **see**.

Phonics

The children should be able to decode the names of the children in the picture.

Phonics activity

Ask the children to correct the sentence below.

i can smel with my nose
The children should add a capital letter to the start and a full stop to the end. Some may also correct the spelling of 'smell'.

2 First steps

Read the text together and then encourage the children to discuss the following questions.

1. **Who is in the picture?**
   Encourage the children to read the names in the picture.

2. **Which is your favourite picture? Why?**
   Answers will vary (e.g. *My favourite picture is of Jack eating the banana because I like bananas; My favourite picture is of Tess smelling the flower because it looks pretty*).

3. **What are the activities shown in the pictures? Which of these activities have you done before?**
   Answers will vary. Encourage the children to name all of the activities. Some may have done them all before; others may have only experienced a few.

3 Explore

- If the children are not learning about senses as part of topic work, it is a good idea to build up their understanding at this point so that they can fully engage with the picture. Point out that we experience the senses by using different parts of our bodies. The BBC Bitesize website has useful videos that explore the senses for children in Key Stage 1. There are more useful resources in the **Reading list**.

- Take the children on a 'senses walk'. Ask them to think about what they can see, smell, touch, hear or even taste as they explore the school, playground or local area. This activity could be completed in a few minutes or it could be a longer excursion, in which case it is a good idea to ask the children to focus on one sense at a time. You may wish to give them clipboards so they can record their observations; alternatively, you could scribe their comments. You could then discuss their findings when you return to the classroom.

4 Skills focus   See pages 34 to 35

Use the information from the **Skills guide** and the relevant **Skills graphic** to introduce the skill of retrieval.

1. Model the skill using the **Unit 2 Modelling slides** and the **Modelling retrieval** guidance on page 34.

2. The children could then attempt the optional **Retrieval** questions on page 38. This may be in small groups with adult support as needed.

Answers and marking guidance for all questions are included on pages 34 to 35.

5 Where next?

- **Speaking and listening task:** Set up five 'sense activities' in the classroom (e.g. tasting different fruits and vegetables; smelling herbs/spices; looking at pictures or videos; comparing textures such as sand, metal and wood; listening to music/playing musical instruments, etc.). Encourage the children to make observations and comparisons as they complete the activities in small groups, focusing on the senses and how they are being used.

- **Writing task:** Ask the children to think about the senses that are being used in the 'sense activities' above. They could record the senses used for each one using the **Activity** resource on page 39.

Reading list

Class reads
- *The Listening Walk* by Paul Showers
- *The Magic School Bus Explores the Senses* by Joanna Cole
- *Your Body, Your Senses* by Peter Riley

Independent reads
- *My Five Senses* by Aliki
- *You Can't Smell a Flower with Your Ear!* by Joanna Cole

Non-fiction
- *How to Really Fool Yourself: Illusions for All Your Senses* by Vicki Cobb
- *My Big Book of the Five Senses* by Patrick George

Poetry
- *Sensational!* by Roger McGough (ed)

TV series
- *Nina and the Neurons* (CBeebies, 2007–2015)

Websites
- The KS1 area of the BBC Bitesize website contains a useful video and interactive game called 'What are the senses?'.
- The CBeebies website has a video of the 'Super Senses Song' from *Nina and the Neurons*.
- The KidsHealth website features lots of ideas for experiments that can be carried out to explore the senses.

Modelling retrieval

▽ See Unit 2 Modelling slides

Use the **Skills guide** (see pages 16 to 17) and the downloadable **Skills graphic** to support your modelling.

1. **Which sense is Tess using? Tick <u>one</u>.**

   taste ☐
   sight ☐
   hearing ☐
   smell ☑

   Explain that to answer retrieval questions, we retrieve (or 'find') the information in the text (or picture, in this case). Explain that you will first identify the key words in the question ('Which'/'sense'/'Tess'/'Tick one') and highlight them. Think aloud: *I need to find Tess in the picture and look at what she is doing.* Encourage the children to read the names and use 'Fastest finger first' (see page 17) to find Tess. Ask them to work in pairs and to tell their partner what Tess is doing. Continue: *Tess is smelling a flower, so she is using her sense of smell. The question tells me to 'tick one', so I will find the word 'smell' in my list and tick it.* Model ticking one answer only and checking it against the question.

2. **Which two children are using their sense of taste?**

   Jack and **Sam**

   Model reading the question and highlighting the key words. Think aloud: *I need to look at the different activities that the children are doing.* Encourage the children to look at the picture and tell their partner which activities use the sense of taste. Emphasise that the question asks for two answers. Continue: *Meg is stroking a cat, so I don't think she is using her sense of taste.* Repeat with the other children, until you come to Jack and Sam: *Jack is eating a banana and Sam is licking a lolly. They are both using taste.* Model copying the names 'Jack' and 'Sam'. Discuss how you retrieved this information by finding their names in the picture. Then model checking the answer against the question.

3. **Which sense is Will using? Tick <u>one</u>.**

   taste ☐
   hearing ☐
   smell ☐
   touch ☑

   Model reading the question and highlighting the key words. Think aloud: *I need to find Will in the picture and look at what he is doing.* Encourage the children to read the names and use 'Fastest finger first' (see page 17) to find Will. Ask them to tell their partner what Will is doing. Continue: *Will must be feeling very cold because he is shivering. He is holding a snowball with his bare hand. This means he is touching snow, so I will tick the word 'touch'.* Model ticking one answer only and checking it against the question.

4. **Draw lines to match the activities to the senses.**

   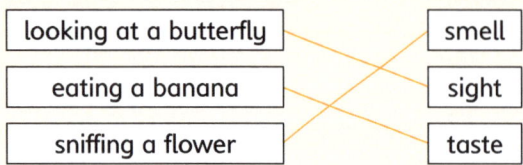

   Model reading the question and highlighting the key words ('Draw lines'/'match'/'activities'/'senses'). Think aloud: *I need to find these three activities in the picture. I am going to put a circle around each one.* Continue: *Looking at a butterfly means that you are using your sense of sight. I will draw a line to 'sight'.* Repeat with the other two activities. When you have finished, model checking that the lines you have drawn are clear.

Retrieval questions mark scheme

See page 38

The following guidance can be used with the children if support is needed.

Answer	Guidance
1 touch ✓	Remind the children to identify the key words in the question and highlight them. Then encourage them to find Meg and look at what she is doing (stroking a cat). Prompt them to identify that she is *touching* the cat. Remind them to tick one answer only. **Award 1 mark for the correct answer ticked.**
2 Kit	Encourage the children to identify the key words in the question and highlight them. Ask them if they can see any activities that involve sounds or listening (e.g. singing or music). Encourage them to identify the name of the child who is doing these activities (Kit) and support them to write it down. **Award 1 mark for the correct answer.**
3 sight ✓	Prompt the children to identify the key words in the question and highlight them. They should then find Ash and discuss what she is doing (looking at a butterfly). Discuss what sense Ash is using and remind the children to tick one answer only. **Award 1 mark for the correct answer ticked.**
4 stroking the cat — hearing singing a song — touch licking a lolly — taste	Encourage the children to identify the key words in the question and highlight them. Support them to find and circle the three activities from the question in the picture. Discuss which sense is being used for each activity. Finally, encourage the children to draw clear lines to show their answers. **Award 1 mark for one pair correctly matched. Award 2 marks for all pairs correctly matched.**

Unit 2

Our Senses

This is a picture of children using their senses. Have you ever used your senses in a similar way to any of the children in the picture? How else have you used your senses?

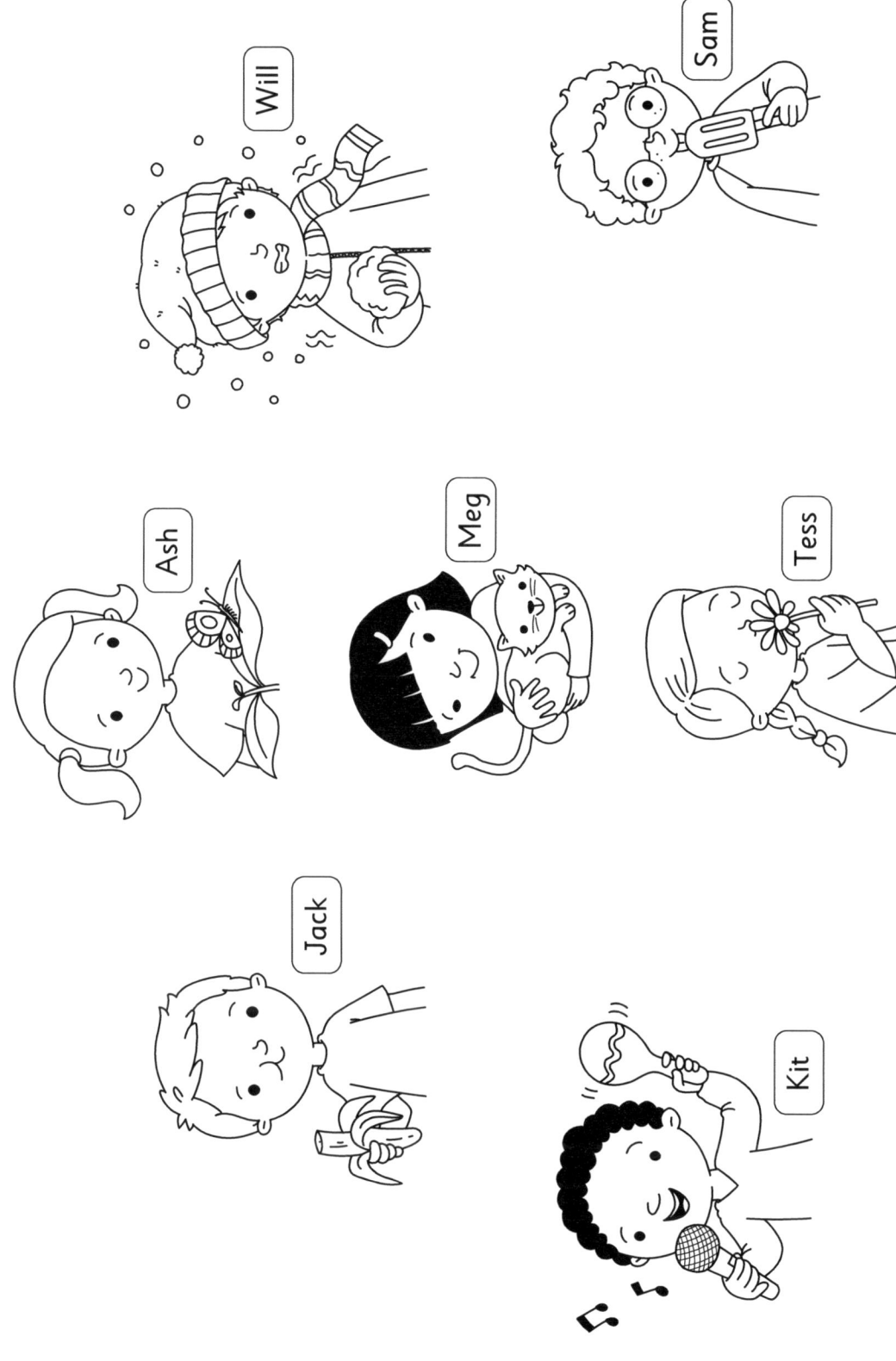

Matching senses

Draw lines to match the sense words to the correct body parts.

sight	hearing	taste	touch	smell
		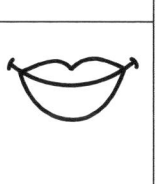	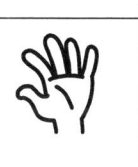	

Unit 2

Retrieval

Name: _____

1 Which sense is Meg using? Tick **one**.

- taste ☐
- touch ☐
- smell ☐
- hearing ☐

1 mark

2 Who is using their sense of hearing?

_____

1 mark

3 Which sense is Ash using? Tick **one**.

- sight ☐
- smell ☐
- touch ☐
- hearing ☐

1 mark

4 Draw lines to match the activities to the correct senses.

stroking the cat	taste
singing a song	touch
licking a lolly	hearing

2 marks

Photocopiable resource from *Complete Comprehension 1* © Schofield & Sims Ltd, 2020.

Activity

Name: _____

What senses do you use for the activities you have explored? Write the activity and the senses used. One has been done for you.

Activity	Senses used
eating a banana	taste, touch, smell

Unit 3 — Retrieval / Poetry

Mary Had a Little Lamb
by Sarah Josepha Hale

▽ **Printable text** • **Modelling slides**   📖 **Photocopiable text and questions** • pages 44 to 47

'Mary Had a Little Lamb' has been chosen as the first comprehension text because it is a nursery rhyme with which many children are familiar. The illustrations support the children's understanding of what is happening in the rhyme. As this is a familiar text, the children are likely to already know some of the words and can therefore focus on the meaning. Nursery rhymes such as this, and 'Jack and Jill' in Unit 4, are important for young children because they help them to develop an understanding of language: the rhyme and rhythm help them to hear the sounds and syllables in words. Nursery rhymes also represent many children's first exposure to poetry. At this stage in the year, the children are likely to respond best to hearing the text read aloud initially.

❶ Get ready

Discuss the **Key vocabulary** identified in the **Language toolkit** and then complete the vocabulary and phonics activities as desired. Please note that the selected vocabulary is a guide. Depending on the needs of your cohort, additional vocabulary discussion may be beneficial before, during and after reading. Next, display the text (pages 44 to 45) so the children can see the title and any illustrations, and encourage the children to discuss the following questions before reading.

1 **What type of text is this?**
   If necessary, you could explain that this is a nursery rhyme, which is a type of rhyming poem that is often sung to or by children.

2 **Have you heard this nursery rhyme before? Where?**
   Answers will vary. Some children may not have heard it until they started school. Other children may have heard it at home or at playgroups.

3 **Look at the picture. What do you think this nursery rhyme is about?**
   The picture shows that this nursery rhyme is about a lamb and a girl.

Language toolkit

Key vocabulary

appear	eager	fleece
followed	lamb	lingered
patiently	teacher	little

Vocabulary discussion questions

- When have you **lingered** somewhere? Who or what were you waiting for?
- What does it mean to wait **patiently**?
- Are you more likely to be **eager** to go to a party or to go to the doctor's?

Vocabulary activities

Discuss which sentence makes the most sense.

1 I **followed** my mum. OR I **followed** a tree.
2 The lamb **lingered** until Mary **appeared**. OR The lamb **lingered** until a **fleece appeared**.

Phonics

Year 1 phonics	children, laugh, near, play, reply, snow, sure
Split digraphs	made, white, rule
Common exception words	go, her, love, one, school, so, the, to, was, you

Phonics activity

Ask the children to correct the sentence below.

mary had a lam wiv a white fleece

The children should add a capital letter to the start and a full stop to the end. Some may also correct the spelling of 'with' and 'lamb'.

② First steps

Read the text together and then encourage the children to discuss the following questions.

1 **Who is the nursery rhyme about?**
   The poem is about a girl called Mary and a lamb.

2 **What does the poet mean by 'turned it out' when talking about what the teacher did?**
   If necessary, support the children to understand that the teacher told the lamb to leave the school. You could discuss whether the same thing would happen if a lamb visited your classroom.

3 **What did you like about the nursery rhyme?**
   Answers will vary. Some may like the nursery rhyme because it is familiar; others may like the poem because it rhymes or because they like the idea of the lamb going to school with Mary.

③ Explore

- This version of 'Mary Had a Little Lamb' may be different from the one that the children know, as it does not include the repetition that features in the sung version (e.g. 'Mary had a little lamb, little lamb, little lamb …'). It may be worth singing the version with the repetitions and linking it to the text. Point out that the text uses the same words as the song but it does not use repetition. Discuss which version the children prefer and why.

- It may be helpful to have a discussion with the children about the fact that there are often many different versions of nursery rhymes and fairy tales. You could explain that this is because they have been told over many years and they were originally told verbally and not written down. Today, they are still spoken aloud and everyone who shares the story may tell it slightly differently.

- To encourage the children to fully engage with the nursery rhyme, you could then play several versions of it using video clips. There are lots of different versions available online, some with different tunes and rhythms. You may want to discuss which version they prefer and why. Before you play a video, decide whether or not to play it with the animations on the screen or if you would prefer the children to only listen to the lyrics. While the animation may help some children, the conversation may then focus on the animation rather than the words of the rhyme.

④ Skills focus   See pages 42 to 43

Use the information from the **Skills guide** and the relevant **Skills graphic** to introduce the skill of retrieval.

1 Model the skill using the **Unit 3 Modelling slides** and the **Modelling retrieval** guidance on page 42.

2 The children could then attempt the optional **Retrieval** questions on page 46. This may be in small groups with adult support as needed.

Answers and marking guidance for all questions are included on pages 42 to 43.

⑤ Where next?

- **Speaking and listening task:** Ask the children to work with a partner to highlight the rhyming words in the text. You could ask them to identify the rhymes verbally first. You may wish to point out that 'rules' and 'school', and 'cried' and 'reply', are half rhymes.

- **Writing task:** Using the **Activity** resource on page 47, the children could use the text to write a simple sentence or phrase to describe what is happening in each picture. You could write some key words on the board to help them get started (e.g. 'walk', 'school', 'follow', 'laugh', 'play', 'tell', 'outside').

Reading list

Class reads
▶ *Mary Had a Dinosaur* by Eileen Browne
▶ *Mary Had a Little Glam* by Tammi Sauer
▶ *Maria Had a Little Llama* by Angela Dominguez
▶ *Mary had a Little Lab* by Sue Fliess

Independent reads
▶ 'Jack and Jill', traditional nursery rhyme (Linked text: Unit 4)

Non-fiction
▶ National Geographic Kids Readers: *Farm Animals* by Joanne Mattern

Poetry
▶ *Classic Nursery Rhymes* by L. Edna Walker (ed)
▶ *A Pop-Up Book of Nursery Rhymes* by Matthew Reinhart

Websites
▶ The CBeebies website has a good selection of nursery-rhyme videos.

Unit 3 · Retrieval · Poetry

Modelling retrieval

▽ See Unit 3 Modelling slides

Use the **Skills guide** (see pages 16 to 17) and the downloadable **Skills graphic** to support your modelling.

1 **What did the children do when the lamb went to school? Tick <u>one</u>.**

jump and skip ☐
laugh and play ☑
clap and shout ☐

Emphasise that the answers to retrieval questions will be found in the text. Model reading the question and highlighting the key words. Think aloud: *First I need to find the part that mentions the children at the school.* You could highlight this text (the second verse) when you find it. Explain that the answer will be found in this part of the text. Continue: *The question tells me to tick one so I need to look at the possible answers.* Model reading them and then rereading the relevant part of the text: *'It made the children laugh and play to see the lamb at school'. The text says, 'laugh and play' and this is one of the possible answers. I know I can only tick one answer.* Model ticking the answer and checking it against the question.

2 **What did the teacher do when she saw the lamb? Tick <u>one</u>.**

invited it in ☐
called the farmer ☐
turned it out ☑

Model reading the question and highlighting the key words. Think aloud: *I need to look near where I looked before because this question is also about the lamb going to school. This time I need to find the part of the text that mentions the teacher.* You could highlight these lines in a different colour than that used for the previous question. As before, model reading the possible answers and rereading the text: *The text says, 'turned it out' and this is one of the options to tick.* (The children will already have discussed this phrase in the **First steps** session.) Model ticking one answer only and checking it against the question.

3 **How did the lamb feel about Mary?**

The lamb loved Mary.

Model reading and highlighting the question as before. Think aloud: *First I need to find the part that talks about how the lamb felt.* Model scanning the whole text looking for a 'feeling' word. Continue: *Here it says 'love', which is a feeling. The children cry, 'Why does the lamb love Mary so?'. I think this means that the lamb loved Mary, so I am going to write this in a sentence.* Model writing the answer and checking it against the question.

4 **Look at the third verse. Why did the lamb linger near the school instead of going in?**

The lamb lingered near the school because the teacher turned it out.

Model reading and highlighting the question as before. Think aloud: *This question has a locator – the third verse. That means I need to look in the third verse to find my answer.* Model using 'Fastest finger first' (see page 17) to locate the correct part of the text. Continue: *Now I need to find the part that says the lamb 'lingered near'.* Model reading the lines before and after this phrase: *The teacher 'turned' the lamb 'out' – I think this is why it lingered nearby. I will write this in a sentence.* Model writing the answer and checking it against the question.

Retrieval questions mark scheme

See page 46

The following guidance can be used with the children if support is needed.

	Answer	Guidance
1	to school ✓	Remind the children that the answers to retrieval questions will be found in the text. Ask them to read the question and highlight any key words that tell them how to answer (e.g. 'followed', 'tick one'). Ask them to use their finger to scan the text for the part where the lamb followed Mary. Then encourage them to scan the text for each of the possible answers. Remind them to tick one answer only. **Award 1 mark for the correct answer ticked.**
2	taking a lamb to school ✓	Prompt the children to read the question and highlight any key words that tell them how to answer (e.g. 'tick one'). Ask them to find 'against the rules' in the text. Again, encourage them to scan the text around this phrase for each of the possible answers. Remind them to tick one answer only. **Award 1 mark for the correct answer ticked.**
3	the teacher	Encourage the children to find the key words in the question (e.g. 'Who') and to identify the part of the question that will help them to find the answer ('Mary loves the lamb'). Remind them to reread the relevant part of the text, scanning for this phrase, before writing their answer. **Award 1 mark for the correct answer.**
4	the lamb	Encourage the children to identify the part of the question that will help them to find the answer ('waited patiently'). Encourage them to reread the relevant part of the text, scanning for this phrase, before writing their answer. **Award 1 mark for the correct answer.**

Mary Had a Little Lamb, by Sarah Josepha Hale

This nursery rhyme is one you may have sung before. It is based on the true story of when a little girl took her lamb to school. Have you ever seen an animal in the school playground before? How do you think you and your friends would react to seeing a lamb in your playground?

Mary had a little lamb,
Its fleece was white as snow;

And everywhere that Mary went
The lamb was sure to go.

It followed her to school one day,
Which was against the rules;

It made the children laugh and play
To see a lamb at school.

And so the teacher turned it out,
But still it lingered near,

And waited patiently about
Till Mary did appear.

Why does the lamb love Mary so?
The eager children cried;

Why, Mary loves the lamb, you know,
The teacher did reply.

From 'Mary Had a Little Lamb', by Sarah Josepha Hale.

Retrieval

Name: _____

1 Where was Mary going when the lamb followed her? Tick **one**.

home ☐

to school ☐

to the shops ☐

1 mark

2 What was against the rules? Tick **one**.

having a lamb ☐

laughing at school ☐

taking a lamb to school ☐

1 mark

3 Who told the children that Mary loved the lamb?

_____

1 mark

4 Who waited patiently?

_____

1 mark

Activity

Name: _____

Write a sentence to explain what each character is doing in the picture.

Mary

_____
_____
_____

The lamb

_____
_____
_____

The children

_____
_____
_____

The teacher

_____
_____
_____

Unit 4

Jack and Jill
(Traditional rhyme)

▽ **Printable text** • **Modelling slides**   📖 **Photocopiable text and questions** • **pages 52 to 55**

Building on the work done in Unit 3, this unit focuses on another well-known nursery rhyme: 'Jack and Jill'. Nursery rhymes are important for young children because they help to develop an understanding of language, and the rhyme and rhythm help them to hear the sounds and syllables in words. This nursery rhyme, which will be familiar to most Year 1 children, is an ideal text to use when starting to explore poetry. At this stage in the year, the children are likely to respond best to hearing the text read aloud initially.

① Get ready

Discuss the **Key vocabulary** identified in the **Language toolkit** and then complete the vocabulary and phonics activities as desired. Please note that the selected vocabulary is a guide. Depending on the needs of your cohort, additional vocabulary discussion may be beneficial before, during and after reading. Next, display the text (pages 52 to 53) so the children can see the title and any illustrations, and encourage the children to discuss the following questions before reading.

1. **What is a nursery rhyme?**
   If necessary, explain that a nursery rhyme is a type of rhyming poem that is often sung to children. You may find it helpful to refer back to Unit 3. You could also mention that many nursery rhymes have hidden meanings or messages.

2. **Have you heard this nursery rhyme before? Where?**
   Answers will vary. Some children may not have heard the rhyme until they started school. Other children may have heard it at home or at playgroups.

3. **Do you like nursery rhymes? Why?**
   Answers will vary (e.g. *I like nursery rhymes because I enjoy singing songs and I like to hear words that rhyme*).

4. **Are nursery rhymes easy to understand?**
   Many children will say that nursery rhymes are easy to understand. You may want to explain that, because nursery rhymes are very old, they do often have some tricky language in them, even though the rhyming, sing-song nature of the words makes them sound simple.

Language toolkit

Key vocabulary

caper	causing	crown
disaster	fetch	pail
trot	tumbling	vinegar

Vocabulary discussion questions

- What part of your body is also called the '**crown**'? Why do you think this is?
- How would someone move if they **trot**?
- What is the opposite of a **disaster**?

Vocabulary activities

Discuss which sentence makes the most sense.

1. The dog liked to run and **caper** in the park. OR He was a **caper**.
2. I filled my **pail** with water. OR My face is a **pail**.

Phonics

Year 1 phonics	down, brown, crown, Jill, hill, fell, caper, paper, cross, plaster, disaster, after, water, fast
Split digraphs	broke, came, home
Common exception words	he, his, she, the, to

Phonics activity

Ask the children to correct the sentence below.

jack fell doun and broke his croun
The children should add a capital letter to the start and a full stop to the end. They should also correct the spelling of the digraph 'ow' in 'down' and 'crown'.

2 First steps

Read the text together and then encourage the children to discuss the following questions.

1. **What happens at the start of the nursery rhyme?**
   At the start of the nursery rhyme, Jack and Jill go up a hill to get some water. You could talk about how people had to collect water in buckets or pails before having taps/running water in their houses. (This is also covered below in **Explore**.)

2. **What happened when Jack fell down?**
   He broke his crown/hurt his head. A discussion about how the word 'crown' means 'head' may be appropriate here depending on how recently the children have discussed the **Key vocabulary**.

3. **How did they mend Jack's head?**
   With vinegar and brown paper. A discussion about this being a Victorian method of treating bumps, bruises and headaches will be helpful for the children. This is also covered below in **Explore**.

4. **What happens at the end of the nursery rhyme?**
   Jill gets into trouble because her mum blames her for letting Jack get hurt.

3 Explore

- Discuss the fact that this nursery rhyme was written a long time ago. Talk to the children about how medicine was different in Victorian times and how they used vinegar and brown paper to cure bumps, bruises and headaches. A discussion about why Jack and Jill had to go to 'fetch a pail of water' would be an interesting concept to explore – they did not have any running water in their house and had to use a well. See the **Reading list** for suggestions of resources that will be helpful for discussing the time period.

- Talk about how we might write the nursery rhyme 'Jack and Jill' if it were set today (e.g. 'Jack and Jill went to the water fountain to refill a bottle of water …').

4 Skills focus   See pages 50 to 51

Use the information from the **Skills guide** and the relevant **Skills graphic** to introduce the skill of word meaning.

1. Model the skill using the **Unit 4 Modelling slides** and the **Modelling word meaning** guidance on page 50.

2. The children could then attempt the optional **Word meaning** questions on page 54. This may be in small groups with adult support as needed.

Answers and marking guidance for all questions are included on pages 50 to 51.

5 Where next?

- **Speaking and listening task:** Using the **Activity** resource on page 55, the children could sequence the events and retell the story to a partner.

- **Writing task:** Using the **Activity** resource on page 55, the children could write two short sentences to retell some of the events from the nursery rhyme, using the word bank to help them.

Reading list

Class reads
- *The Orchard Book of Nursery Rhymes* by Zena Sutherland and Faith Jaques
- *The Puffin Book of Nursery Rhymes* by Raymond Briggs
- *Usborne Illustrated Book of Nursery Rhymes* by Felicity Brooks

Independent reads
- 'Mary Had a Little Lamb' by Sarah Josepha Hale (Linked text: Unit 3)
- *Mixed Up Nursery Rhymes* by Hilary Robinson

Non-fiction
- *100 Facts: Victorian Britain* by Jeremy Smith

Poetry
- 'Jack and Jill' by Kate Willis-Crowley
- *Nursery Rhymes* by Debi Gliori
- *Tadpoles Nursery Rhymes: Jack and Jill/Jack and Jill Go Skating* by Wes Magee

Websites
- The Topmarks website has a good selection of educational resources about living in Victorian Britain.

Unit 4

Modelling word meaning

> See Unit 4 Modelling slides

Use the **Skills guide** (see pages 14 to 15) and the downloadable **Skills graphic** to support your modelling.

1 **Which word from the nursery rhyme means 'head'? Tick <u>one</u>.**

   pail ☐
   crown ☑
   fetch ☐

   Model rereading the poem, scanning for each of the possible answers in the text and highlighting them. Then model replacing each of the words with 'head' (e.g. 'to fetch a *head* of water'; 'and broke his *head*'; 'to *head* a pail of water'). Point out that the question asks for one answer only to be ticked. Discuss which answer makes the most sense. You could encourage the children to refer to the illustrations. Model ticking one answer only and checking it against the question.

2 **Find and copy <u>one</u> word from the first verse that means 'bucket'.**

   pail

   Explain that this is similar to the first question, but instead of ticking a box we have to find the answer in the text and write it down. Emphasise that the answer should be one word only. Think aloud: *Which word in the poem would make sense if we replaced it with the word 'bucket'?* Model noticing the locator and highlighting the relevant part of the text: *I need to look at the first verse of the poem. Here it says 'To fetch a pail of water'. It makes sense to fetch a 'bucket' of water, so the answer must be 'pail'.* Model writing the answer and checking it against the question.

3 **Draw lines to match the words to their meanings.**

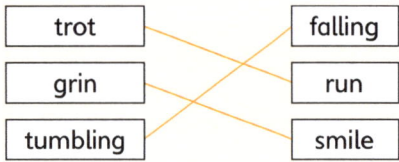

   Ask the children to look at the left-hand column of three words. Explain that they may already know what these words mean but that it is best to double-check them in the text as words can have many different meanings. Model highlighting the three words in the text and discussing, in turn, which other words would make sense in their place. Discuss which of the words on the right the children would choose for each one. Model matching up the answers and checking them against the question. When you have finished, model checking that the lines you have drawn are clear.

4 **Which group of words tells us that Jill got into trouble?**

   told her off

   Think aloud: *First I need to find the parts in the poem where Jill is mentioned. I won't reread the entire poem; instead, I will use my finger to scan for the word 'Jill'. Here it says, 'Jill came tumbling after', but that doesn't mean she got into trouble.* As you model scanning for 'Jill' in the rest of the rhyme, continue: *It says that Jill grinned, but that doesn't mean she got into trouble either. I will read on … Here it says, 'Mother, cross, told her off'. 'Her' must be Jill. This means that Jill got into trouble with her mother. Reading on, I can see that Jill's mother was angry because she blamed Jill for causing Jack's accident. I think the group of words I need is 'told her off'.* Model writing the answer and checking it against the question.

Jack and Jill (Traditional rhyme)

Word meaning questions mark scheme

See page 54

The following guidance can be used with the children if support is needed.

	Answer	Guidance
1	caper ✓	Ask the children to find the key words in the question. Then ask them to find the three possible answers in the text and talk about what each word means. Remind them to tick one answer only. **Award 1 mark for the correct answer ticked.**
2	disaster	Discuss what the word 'accident' means and think about which word from the text would be the closest in meaning. You may want to prompt the children by asking *Who has an accident in this rhyme?* (Jack). Encourage them to scan for Jack's name in the text, looking for a word that describes what happened to him. Remind them to answer with one word only. **Award 1 mark for the correct answer.**
3	caper — fix mend — move cross — angry (caper–fix, mend–move, cross–angry; with caper crossing to fix and mend to move)	Remind the children to find the three words in the left-hand column in the text and discuss, in turn, which other words have a similar meaning. Then ask them to choose which of the words in the right-hand column would make sense in their place. Finally, support them to draw clear lines to show their answers. **Award 1 mark for one pair correctly matched. Award 2 marks for all pairs correctly matched.**
4	cross	Encourage the children to scan for the line of the text that mentions Jack and Jill's mother. They should then scan for a word that describes a feeling. Remind them to answer with one word only. **Award 1 mark for the correct answer.**

Jack and Jill

This is a nursery rhyme that you may have heard or sung before, but do you know all the verses and do you understand what they mean?

Jack and Jill went up the hill,

To fetch a pail of water;

Jack fell down, and broke his crown

And Jill came tumbling after.

Up Jack got and home did trot

As fast as he could caper;

He went to bed to mend his head
With vinegar and brown paper.

Jill came in and she did grin,
To see his paper plaster.

Mother, cross, told her off,
For causing Jack's disaster.

Word meaning

Name: _____

1 Which word means 'move'? Tick **one**.

pail ☐

caper ☐

vinegar ☐

1 mark

2 Find and copy **one** word that means 'accident'.

_____

1 mark

3 Draw lines to match the words to their meanings.

caper		fix
mend		move
cross		angry

2 marks

4 Find and copy **one** word that tells you how Mother was feeling about Jill.

_____

1 mark

Activity

Name: _____

Write a number in each box to put the pictures in order. One has been done for you. Then retell the story to your partner.

Write some sentences to explain what happened. Use the word bank to help you.

First _____

Then _____

Word bank

| Jack | Jill | pail | water | fell | trot | head | Mother | cross |

Unit 5

Snow Bear
by Tony Mitton

▽ **Printable text** • **Modelling slides**   📖 **Photocopiable text and questions** • **pages 60 to 63**

Inference

Snow Bear is the first comprehension text taken from a popular children's book. It is written in rhyme, which provides a useful link to the nursery rhymes in Units 3 and 4. In this text, Snow Bear is trying to find somewhere to sleep but with no luck. You could use this text to make links to the topics of seasons and weather in the Year 1 science curriculum. The subject matter also links closely to the text in Unit 6: *Can't You Sleep, Little Bear?*. At this stage in the year, the children are likely to respond best to hearing the text read aloud initially.

❶ Get ready

Discuss the **Key vocabulary** identified in the **Language toolkit** and then complete the vocabulary and phonics activities as desired. Please note that the selected vocabulary is a guide. Depending on the needs of your cohort, additional vocabulary discussion may be beneficial before, during and after reading. Next, display the text (pages 60 to 61) so the children can see the title and any illustrations, and encourage the children to discuss the following questions before reading.

1 **What type of text is this and how do you know?**
   I think this text is a story because of the title and because the pictures of the bear look like they come from a story rather than a non-fiction text. Some children may think this text is another nursery rhyme. Explain that it is from a made-up, or fictional, story that is written in rhyme.

2 **Looking at the picture, what do you think the story is about?**
   I think it is about a fox and a bear who meet in the snow.

3 **Have you ever seen snow? What was it like?**
   *Answers will vary according to the children's experiences (e.g. 'cold', 'wet', 'slippery', 'pretty'). See **Explore** and **Where next?** for activity ideas for any children who have never seen snow.*

Language toolkit

Key vocabulary

growls	gruff	litter
plods	sighs	sorry
spare	trudges	world

Vocabulary discussion questions

- What have you said **sorry** for?
- What are the different meanings of **litter**?
- How would someone move if they **trudge** or **plod**? (You could encourage the children to act these movements out.)

Vocabulary activities

Discuss which sentence makes the most sense.

1 The dog **growls** at the cat. OR
   The fish **growls** at the cat.

2 There are many countries in the **world**. OR
   There are no countries in the **world**.

Phonics

Year 1 phonics	dark, warm, bear, cold, chicks, sight, dry, cosy, deep, sleep, tree, free, farmhouse
Split digraphs	place, white, hole, home
Common exception words	are, come, has, his, no, so, there, to, you

Phonics activity

Ask the children to correct the sentence below.

one winter it began 2 snow

The children should add a capital letter to the start and add a full stop to the end. They should also change '2' to 'to'.

Fiction

Unit 5 — Inference — Fiction

2 First steps

Read the text together and then encourage the children to discuss the following questions.

1. **What time of year, or season, is the story set in? How do you know?**
   It is set in winter because it is cold and snowy. Some children may refer to the illustrations. Others may refer to the phrase 'cold world of white'.

2. **Who is in the story?**
   Snow Bear, Fox and Owl.

3. **What is Snow Bear trying to do in the story?**
   Answers will vary. Many children will say that Snow Bear is trying to find somewhere to sleep but the places he finds already have other animals living in them. Some children may use the skill of inference to add that he wants somewhere to sleep because he is cold in the snow and tired of walking.

3 Explore

- All children, especially those who have not experienced snow, will benefit from a sensory activity to help them identify with the themes of the text. If it is a cold day, wrap up warm and go outside. Ask the children to work with a partner to think of words to describe the cold (e.g. 'cold', 'cool', 'icy', 'freezing', 'frozen', 'chilly', 'frosty', 'bitter', 'glacial', 'polar'). Scribe their ideas: you could supply some of the example words as prompts if needed. As a class, discuss the children's words and order them from strongest to weakest. You could relate these words to how Snow Bear is feeling out in the snow. (If it is not a cold day, you may want to use some iced water and ask the children to briefly dip their fingers in it, before continuing the activity as above.)

- You could extend the activity above by asking the children to describe how they feel when they come back inside (e.g. 'warm', 'toasty', 'hot', 'comfortable', 'pleasant', 'relaxed', 'snug', 'cosy'). As above, discuss and order the words they contribute, relating them to the conditions that Snow Bear is trying to find in the story.

- You could share photographs and videos of snow, ice and cold environments to help them engage with the text and encourage them to relate to how the animals feel in the story.

4 Skills focus — See pages 58 to 59

Use the information from the **Skills guide** and the relevant **Skills graphic** to introduce the skill of inference.

1. Model the skill using the **Unit 5 Modelling slides** and the **Modelling inference** guidance on page 58.

2. If desired, the children could then attempt the optional **Inference** questions on page 62. This may be in small groups with adult support as needed.

Answers and marking guidance for all questions are included on pages 58 to 59.

5 Where next?

- **Speaking and listening task:** Using props such as soft toys or pictures, ask the children to retell the story to support their understanding of story features. You could prompt them to predict what might happen next in the story and act it out for you (e.g. Who do they think might live in the farmhouse? Will they help Snow Bear?).

- **Writing task:** Try creating some synthetic snow to help stimulate the children's senses before completing the **Activity** resource on page 63. To make the snow, pour one cup of baking soda in a bowl and slowly add in shaving cream until you are happy with the consistency. The 'snow' stays cool to the touch and has a powder-like feel. You could also provide ice cubes for the children to touch. Encourage them to generate adjectives to describe the 'snow' and how it feels.

Reading list

Class reads
- *Lost in the Snow* by Holly Webb
- *One Snowy Night* by Nick Butterworth

Independent reads
- *Can't You Sleep, Little Bear?* by Martin Waddell (Linked text: Unit 6)
- *Kipper's Snowy Day* by Mick Inkpen
- *Tiger in the Snow!* by Nick Butterworth

Non-fiction
- *All About Animals in Winter* by Martha E. H. Rustad
- *Animals in Winter* by H. Bancroft and R. Van Gelder
- *A Bed for the Winter* by Karen Wallace
- *Secrets of Winter* by Carron Brown and Georgina Tee
- *Tree: Seasons Come, Seasons Go* by Patricia Hegarty
- *When Winter Comes* by Pearl Neuman

Poetry
- *It's Snowing! It's Snowing! Winter Poems* by Jack Prelutsky

Websites
- The CBeebies website has a helpful quiz about hibernating animals.

Modelling inference

See Unit 5 Modelling slides

Use the **Skills guide** (see pages 20 to 21) and the downloadable **Skills graphic** to support your modelling.

1. **Why do you think Snow Bear wants to find a place to sleep? Tick one.**

   It is warm outside. ☐
   It is cold outside. ☑
   It is breezy outside. ☐
   It is sunny outside. ☐

   Emphasise that the answers to inference questions are not found in the text; you need to use clues from the text to work them out. Read the question together and highlight the key words. Think aloud: *'Why do you think' means that we need to think about the information in the text to work out the answer. I need to use the key words in the question and look for where the text first mentions that Snow Bear is looking for a place to sleep. Then I need to think about which one of the possible answers explains why. Here it says, 'a place where a cold bear could sleep'.* Continue: *Let's think back to times when we have felt cold. I know I wouldn't want to stay outside if I felt cold.* If necessary, you could discuss the meaning of 'warm', 'cold', 'breezy' and 'sunny'. Model ticking one answer only and checking it against the question.

2. **How do you know that Fox feels bad that there is no room for Snow Bear?**

   I know he feels bad for Snow Bear because he says he is sorry.

   Model reading the question and highlighting the key words. Point out that this question asks: 'How do you know?', so you need to explain the clues you find in the text. Think aloud: *First I need to find where it mentions Fox in the text.* Encourage the children to help you. Continue: *Now I need to think about why Fox might feel bad for Snow Bear. There is no room in Fox's hole because his litter of cubs are in there. It says here that Fox growls – growling might not sound friendly, but that might just be the way Fox talks, and he does say, "I'm sorry".* Continue: *I think Fox says sorry because he feels bad that there is no room in the hole for Snow Bear. Now I need to write my answer as a sentence.* Model writing the answer and encourage the children to help you. Model checking the answer against the question.

3. **True or false? When Snow Bear finds a hole in a tree, there is enough room to sleep there. Explain your answer.**

   False – Owl and her chicks are in the hole.

   If necessary, discuss the meaning of 'true' and 'false'. Ask the children to help you find and highlight the event in the story. Think aloud: *Snow Bear does find a hole in the tree but Owl tells him that her chicks are in the hole and there is no more room.* Encourage the children to discuss what this means and how they would use this to answer the question. Continue: *The answer is false, because Owl and her chicks are in the hole and Owl tells Snow Bear that there is no room for him.* Model writing the answer and encourage the children to help you. Model checking the answer against the question.

4. **Reread the verse that begins *Snow Bear just sighs*. How do you know that Snow Bear is upset about having nowhere to stay? Explain your answer.**

   The text says, '"Oh for a home!" is his sad little song'.

   Model using the locator to find the right verse. Ask the children to reread it and highlight the key words in the question. Think aloud: *Snow Bear sighs. Often people sigh when they are sad. However, I need to read the rest of the verse to look for more clues.* Encourage the children to read on and discuss with their partners. Continue: *The text says, '"Oh, for a home!" is his sad little song'. I think this is how we know Snow Bear is upset about having nowhere to stay – he says he wishes he had a home in a sad voice. I now need to write this in a sentence to answer the question.* Model writing the answer with the children's input and checking it against the question.

Inference questions mark scheme

See page 62

The following guidance can be used with the children if support is needed.

	Answer	Guidance
1	Inside it is warm and dry. ✓	Remind the children that the answers to inference questions are not found in the text; they will need to use clues from the text to work them out. If necessary, encourage them to identify the key words in the question. Then prompt them to use the locator and look at the first verse. Ask them to think about why Snow Bear would choose a hole to sleep in. Can they find any clues in the text ('dark, dry and deep')? Encourage them to look at the possible answers and find the answer that best matches what they know from the text. Remind them to tick one answer only. **Award 1 mark for the correct answer ticked.**
2	He is upset. ✓	Encourage the children to identify the key words in the question. Then prompt them to find where Owl tells Snow Bear that there is no room. If further support is needed, discuss how Snow Bear is feeling outside and that he has already been turned away from one hole. Ask the children to think about how they would feel if they were Snow Bear. Remind them to tick one answer only. **Award 1 mark for the correct answer ticked.**
3	True – he tries two different holes before he sees the farmhouse.	Discuss the meaning of 'true' and 'false'. Encourage the children to discuss what the question is asking and what 'tries hard' means (is determined, doesn't give up). Discuss how Snow Bear shows this in the text (he tries to find shelter in one hole and then he tries another). You could ask the children to think about how they try hard and don't give up – even if a task is challenging – when they do something in school and relate this to Snow Bear's experience. **Award 1 mark for 'true' and any reference to Snow Bear trying more than one place.**
4	Snow Bear feels excited.	Encourage the children to first highlight the key words in the question and then find the part of the text that mentions the farmhouse. Remind them that Snow Bear is sad and cold but he has just seen a warm farmhouse – how would that make him feel? More able children may mention the exclamation mark in 'But look!' and this may help in understanding that Snow Bear is excited. **Award 1 mark for any reference to Snow Bear being excited/ happy/enthusiastic/glad.**

Snow Bear, by Tony Mitton

Have you ever been really cold at night-time? What did you do to warm up? Imagine if you had nowhere to sleep and it was snowing outside – what would you do? In this text, Snow Bear is looking for somewhere to sleep away from the snow, but he can't find anywhere.

He's spotted a hole, and it's dark, dry and deep,

Perhaps it's a place where a cold bear could sleep?

"Oh, I'm sorry," growls Fox, "but there's no room to spare.

It's my den, and my litter of cubs is down there."

Snow Bear plods on to a crooked old tree.

There's a warm, cosy hole in it – could it be free?

But tufty gruff Owl hoots, "Tu-whit!" and "Tu-whoo!

My chicks are in there so there's no room for you."

Snow Bear just sighs. Then he trudges along.
"Oh, for a home!" is his sad little song.

But look! A small farmhouse has come into sight,
a place that looks warm in this cold world of white.

From *Snow Bear* by Tony Mitton, copyright ©2015 Tony Mitton. Published by Bloomsbury Publishing Plc.

Inference

Name: _____

1 Why do you think that Snow Bear thinks Fox's hole is a good place to sleep? Tick **one**.

In Fox's hole, it is windy and blustery. ☐

In Fox's hole, it is wet and cold. ☐

In Fox's hole, it is icy and chilly. ☐

In Fox's hole, it is warm and dry. ☐

1 mark

2 How does Snow Bear feel when Owl tells him he can't sleep in the tree? Tick **one**.

He is upset. ☐

He is happy. ☐

He is bored. ☐

He is excited. ☐

1 mark

3 True or false? Snow Bear tries hard to find a place to sleep. Explain your answer.

_____

_____

1 mark

4 How do you think Snow Bear feels when he sees the farmhouse?

_____

_____

1 mark

Activity

Name: _____

What does snow feel like when you touch it? Write words on the lines to describe how it feels. Use the word bank or your own ideas.

Word bank

| warm | hard | soft | crunchy | wet | icy | cold | frozen | dry | hot |

_____

_____

_____

Unit 5

Snow Bear, by Tony Mitton

Photocopiable resource from *Complete Comprehension 1* © Schofield & Sims Ltd, 2020.

Unit 6

Can't You Sleep, Little Bear?
by Martin Waddell

▽ **Printable text** • **Modelling slides**   📖 **Photocopiable text and questions** • **pages 68 to 71**

The theme of this well-loved story is one that all children can relate to – settling down at bedtime. Martin Waddell's stories are highly popular with this age group – there is another to enjoy in *Progress check 1*. At this stage in the year, the children are likely to respond best to hearing the text read aloud initially.

Word meaning

① Get ready

Discuss the **Key vocabulary** identified in the **Language toolkit** and then complete the vocabulary and phonics activities as desired. Please note that the selected vocabulary is a guide. Depending on the needs of your cohort, additional vocabulary discussion may be beneficial before, during and after reading. Next, display the text (pages 68 to 69) so the children can see the title and any illustrations, and encourage the children to discuss the following questions before reading.

1 **What sort of text do you think this is?**
   I think the text is a story because of the title and the picture of a bear. Support the children to understand that a made-up story is a type of fiction.

2 **Have you ever had a night where you haven't been able to sleep? What happened?**
   Answers will vary depending on the children's experiences.

3 **What do you do every night to get ready for bed?**
   A discussion about having a good bedtime routine would be relevant here (e.g. brushing your teeth; listening to bedtime stories; going to bed at the same time each night; having a favourite soft toy or a night-light).

4 **Have you read any stories that you think may be similar?**
   The children may refer to other stories about bears, such as *Whatever Next* by Jill Murphy or fairy tales such as 'Goldilocks and the Three Bears', or stories about being unable to sleep.

Language toolkit

Key vocabulary

bear	bright	cupboard
lantern	little	sleep
sunlight	tiny	tried

Vocabulary discussion questions

- When have you **tried** hard?
- What is the difference between something **little** and something **tiny**?
- What do we use instead of **lanterns** to light our classroom?

Vocabulary activities

Discuss which sentence makes the most sense.

1 **Sunlight** is dark. OR **Sunlight** is bright.
2 The **little bear** was **tiny**. OR
   The big **bear** was **tiny**.

Phonics

Year 1 phonics	dark, glow, part, read, took
igh	light, night
Split digraphs	came, cave, like, home
Common exception words	he, is, once, said, the, there, to, were, you
–ing/–ed suffix	cuddling, getting, padding, looked, played, scared
Contractions	can't, don't, I'm, there's

Phonics activity

Ask the children to correct the sentence below.

the nyt time was dark but the daytime was lit
The children should add a capital letter to the start and add a full stop to the end. They should also correct the spelling of 'night' and 'light'.

Fiction

Schofield & Sims Complete Comprehension 1

2 First steps

Read the text together and then encourage the children to discuss the following questions.

1. **Who is in this story?**
   The characters are Little Bear and Big Bear. You could discuss that Little Bear is the child and Big Bear is the adult.

2. **Why can't Little Bear sleep?**
   Little Bear doesn't like the dark.

3. **We have only read part of the story. What do you think will happen next?**
   Encourage the children to have a go at predicting what they think might happen, as this will help them to engage with the extract.

3 Explore

- Discuss whether or not the children like sleeping in the dark. Emphasise that there is no right or wrong answer: some people like to sleep with a light on, whereas others like it to be pitch black.

- It is darker at some points in the year than at others. Encourage the children to think of the times of year when it is darker for longer (autumn and winter) and why this might be (in winter, our side of the world tilts away from the sun, resulting in fewer hours of sunshine and shorter days).

- Discuss events that are more exciting because they happen in the dark (e.g. Bonfire Night, Halloween, New Year's Eve, Diwali, other festivals of light). As a class, with you scribing, think about the activities that take place at each event and how the children would feel at each celebration. This activity will prepare the children to complete the **Activity** resource on page 71.

4 Skills focus   See pages 66 to 67

Use the information from the **Skills guide** and the relevant **Skills graphic** to introduce the skill of word meaning.

1. Model the skill using the **Unit 6 Modelling slides** and the **Modelling word meaning** guidance on page 66.

2. The children could then attempt the optional **Word meaning** questions on page 70. This may be in small groups with adult support as needed.

Answers and marking guidance for all questions are included on pages 66 to 67.

5 Where next?

- **Speaking and listening task:** The children could work in pairs to retell the story, with one child playing the role of Little Bear and the other playing Big Bear. You could provide them with pictures of bears or masks to help them to get into character.

- **Writing task:** Using the **Activity** resource on page 71, the children could name and discuss some activities that happen when it's dark and write how they feel about each one, with the help of the word bank (e.g. they might feel excited on Bonfire Night, but tired at bedtime).

Reading list

Class reads
- *Bear Snores On* by Karma Wilson
- *The Fox in the Dark* by Alison Green
- *One Snowy Night* by Nick Butterworth
- *The Owl Who Was Afraid of the Dark* by Jill Tomlinson
- *Snow Bear* by Tony Mitton (Linked text: Unit 5)
- *Who's Afraid of the Dark?* by Melanie Joyce

Independent reads
- *Flashlight* by Lizi Boyd (wordless picture book)
- *Owl Babies* by Martin Waddell
- *Whatever Next!* by Jill Murphy

Non-fiction
- *Animals at Night* by Anne Jankeliowitch
- *Little Owl's Night* by Divya Srinivasan
- *When the Stars Come Out* by Nicola Edwards

Poetry
- *A Poem for Every Night of the Year* by Allie Esiri (ed)

Websites
- The BBC Bitesize website contains a fun 'Seymour Science' video about day and night aimed at Key Stage 1 children.
- The BBC website features a clip called 'Nocturnal animals and birds' from *Our Planet*.

 **Modelling word meaning** ▽ See Unit 6 Modelling slides

Use the **Skills guide** (see pages 14 to 15) and the downloadable **Skills graphic** to support your modelling.

1 **Which word in the story tells you that one of the bears is small? Circle <u>one</u>.**

   [little] (circled)   [miniature]   [big]

   Model reading the question and highlighting the key words. Think aloud: *I need to draw a circle round the word that means the same as 'small' and that is in the text.* Model looking at the possible answers and discussing what they mean. You could explain that 'miniature' is a longer form of the word 'mini'. Continue: *I know that 'big' is the opposite of 'small' so it can't be that. The other two words both mean 'small', but I can't tick both.* Model looking back at the text to find which word is used: *The text says 'little' but it doesn't say 'miniature', so the answer must be 'little'. Now I will draw a circle around my answer.* Model circling one answer only and checking it against the question.

2 **Find and copy <u>one</u> word from the story that tells you that the sun was strong.**
   bright

   Think aloud: *I need to look for the part of the text that talks about the sun.* Model scanning the text and think aloud: *Here it says Big Bear and Little Bear 'played all day in the bright sunlight', so the answer must be around this part of the text – we know that they played together until the sun went down.* Continue: *If the sun is strong, that usually means that it is shining very brightly, and in the story it is called 'bright sunlight'. I think 'bright' must be the word I need.* Model writing the answer and checking it against the question.

3 **Draw lines to match the words to their meanings.**

   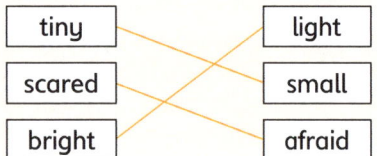

   Ask the children to find the three words from the left-hand column in the text and highlight them. Discuss which of the words on the right they would match to the words on the left. Model trying out each word: *'Tiny' is used to describe the lantern; it means 'little' or 'small'. I will draw a line to match 'tiny' to 'small'.* Repeat for the other two words. Model matching up the answers and checking them against the question. When you have finished, model checking that the lines you have drawn are clear.

4 **Why do you think the author used the word *padding* to describe how Big Bear walks over to the bed?**
   Big Bear has large paws which make a soft, dull noise as he walks.

   Encourage the children to help you find the relevant part of the text. Discuss what 'padding' means. Explain that it has more than one meaning and can refer to when something (e.g. a cushion or soft toy) is filled with stuffing. However, in this case it refers to the way Big Bear moves. Prompt the children to think about how a big bear might move (you could ask them to act it out or watch a video of a bear walking). Explain: *In this text, the word 'padding' means to plod or walk slowly, making a soft, dull noise.* Think aloud: *Why might the author use this word?* Support the children to construct an answer orally before modelling how to write it in a full sentence and check it when complete.

Word meaning questions mark scheme

See page 70

The following guidance can be used with the children if support is needed.

	Answer	Guidance
1	tiniest ✓	Remind the children to scan the text for the part that mentions the lantern and look at the words around it. You could point out that although 'small' also means 'little', it cannot be the answer because the answer must come from the text. Remind the children to tick one answer only. **Award 1 mark for the correct answer ticked.**
2	scared	Ask the children to look at the part of the text where Little Bear talks about how he is feeling. Encourage them to think about where this might be in the text and support them to find the part where Little Bear tells Big Bear how he feels about the dark. Ask: *Can you find a word that describes how Little Bear is feeling?* Remind the children to answer with one word only. **Award 1 mark for the correct answer.**
3	lamp ✓	Support the children to find the part of the text that refers to the lantern and look at the words that describe it. Encourage them to think about what the lantern is used for in the text. Remind them to tick one word only. **Award 1 mark for the correct answer ticked.**
4	big	Encourage the children to think of words that mean the same as 'large'. Then ask them to look at the text to see if they can find one of these words. Remind them to answer with one word only. **Award 1 mark for the correct answer.**

Can't You Sleep, Little Bear?, by Martin Waddell

Have you ever gone to bed and not been able to sleep? Why couldn't you sleep? How did you get to sleep in the end? In this extract, Little Bear can't sleep. There is dark all around him in the Bear Cave. Can Big Bear find a way to help Little Bear fall fast asleep?

Once there were two bears, Big Bear and Little Bear.

Big Bear is the big bear, and Little Bear is the little bear. They played all day in the bright sunlight. When night came, and the sun went down, Big Bear took Little Bear home to the Bear Cave.

Big Bear put Little Bear to bed in the dark part of the cave. "Go to sleep, Little Bear," he said. And Little Bear tried.

Big Bear settled in the Bear Chair and read his Bear Book by the light of the fire. But Little Bear couldn't get to sleep.

"Can't you sleep, Little Bear?" asked Big Bear, putting down his Bear Book (which was just getting to the interesting part) and padding over to the bed.

"I'm scared," said Little Bear.

"Why are you scared, Little Bear?" asked Big Bear.

"I don't like the dark," said Little Bear.

"What dark?" said Big Bear.

"The dark all around us," said Little Bear.

Big Bear looked, and saw that the dark part of the cave was very dark, so he went to the Lantern Cupboard and took out the tiniest lantern that was there.

Big Bear lit the tiniest lantern, and put it near to Little Bear's bed.

"There's a tiny light to stop you being scared, Little Bear," said Big Bear.

"Thank you, Big Bear," said Little Bear, cuddling up in the glow.

"Now go to sleep, Little Bear," said Big Bear, and he padded back to the Bear Chair and settled down to read the Bear Book by the light of the fire.

Little Bear tried to sleep, but he couldn't.

Word meaning

Name: _____

1 Which word in the story tells you that the lantern is little? Tick **one**.

small ☐

massive ☐

tiniest ☐

1 mark

2 Find and copy **one** word that shows that Little Bear is feeling afraid.

_____

1 mark

3 What could be another word for *lantern*? Tick **one**.

jug ☐

fire ☐

lamp ☐

1 mark

4 Find and copy **one** word that means the same as 'large'.

_____

1 mark

Activity

Name: _____

Write the event that is happening in each picture. Use the word bank to help you. Then write down how you would feel at each event.

_____

_____

_____

_____

_____

_____

_____

_____

Word bank

| Bonfire Night | Halloween | bedtime | Diwali |
| sleepy | happy | excited | scared |

Unit 7 — Inference — Fiction

Little Red
by Jo Gray

▽ **Printable text** • **Modelling slides**   📖 **Photocopiable text and questions** • **pages 76 to 79**

'Little Red Riding Hood' is a popular fairy tale with many children. The story has been adapted to allow them to apply their phonic knowledge to read the text more independently, perhaps working in mixed-ability pairs. In this version, Little Red loves roller-skating. She remembers to ask permission to visit her granny but forgets her mother's warning about not talking to strangers. This text is a good starting point for discussions about traditional tales that have a moral message.

① Get ready

Discuss the **Key vocabulary** identified in the **Language toolkit** and then complete the vocabulary and phonics activities as desired. Please note that the selected vocabulary is a guide. Depending on the needs of your cohort, additional vocabulary discussion may be beneficial before, during and after reading. Next, display the text (pages 76 to 77) so the children can see the title and any illustrations, and encourage the children to discuss the following questions before reading.

1. **Look at the picture. What type of text is this? How do you know?**
   Answers will vary (e.g. *I think this is a fairy tale because I can see Little Red Riding Hood in the picture; I think this is a fairy tale because there is a wolf in the picture and I have read fairy tales about wolves before*). Support the children to understand that a fairy tale is a type of fiction.

2. **Which stories do you know that are similar?**
   Answers will vary (e.g. *I have read 'Little Red Riding Hood' and I think this may be a similar story. I also know the story of 'The Three Little Pigs', which has a wolf in it*). You could discuss that, just like nursery rhymes (see Units 3 and 4), fairy tales exist in many different versions as they are such well-known stories.

3. **Looking at the picture, who do you think is in this story?**
   The picture shows us that there is a girl and a wolf. If the children already know 'Little Red Riding Hood', they may be able to name the mother, the granny and the woodcutter.

4. **What do you think will happen in this story?**
   Answers will vary (e.g. *I think that the little girl and the wolf will become friends; I think the wolf will be mean to the girl*). If the children have heard the story of 'Little Red Riding Hood', then they may retell it.

Language toolkit

Key vocabulary

different	little	live
riding	scary	scream
strangers	woodcutter	better

Vocabulary discussion questions

- What was the last thing you found **scary**?
- What makes you **different** from your friends?
- Is a **stranger** somebody you know?

Vocabulary activities

Discuss which sentence makes the most sense.

1. I **screamed** when I baked a cake. OR
   I **screamed** when I saw the wolf.
2. A **woodcutter** chopped down a tree. OR
   A **woodcutter** chopped down a cake.

Phonics

Year 1 phonics	girl, short, talk, wood
Split digraphs	ate, brave, cake, cape, chased, made, plate, skate, takes, nice
Common exception words	house, my, once, said, she, there, was, where

Phonics activity

Ask the children to correct the sentence below.

she wos a brayv girl

The children should add a capital letter to the start and a full stop to the end. They should also correct the spelling of 'was' and the split digraph in 'brave'.

2 First steps

Read the text together and then encourage the children to discuss the following questions.

1 What does Little Red make at the start of the story?
   Little Red makes a cake to take to her granny.

2 How does Little Red get to Granny's house?
   Little Red skates through the woods.

3 What does the wolf do when he gets to Granny's house?
   The wolf eats Granny, puts on her clothes and gets in her bed. The wolf pretends to be Granny.

4 What happens at the end of the story?
   The woodcutter hits the wolf on the head and the wolf runs away. Little Red says sorry to her mum and then they eat the cake that Little Red made.

5 What was your favourite part of the story?
   Any answer is acceptable here as long as it is an event from the story.

3 Explore

- In pairs, the children could use the text to practise and perform the conversations between the wolf and Little Red. You could help the children to highlight the direct speech in the text before they start. Ask: *How would Little Red speak? How would the wolf speak?* Afterwards, the children could swap roles and repeat.

- Discuss how 'Little Red' is similar to and different from other fairy tales that the children know. A similarity might be that fairy tales often have heroes, villains and magic, and in 'Little Red' there is a talking wolf. Fairy tales also sometimes have a message – in 'Little Red', the message is 'Don't talk to strangers'. Can the children think of any other fairy tales that have a moral message? For example, by the end of the story of 'Beauty and the Beast', the Beast is a good man even though he looks like a monster. A difference might be that fairy tales also often include princes and princesses, but 'Little Red' is mostly about ordinary people.

- Challenge the children to think of other fairy tales in which children go walking in the woods by themselves. (Examples are 'Snow White', 'Hansel and Gretel' and 'The Snow Queen'.) You could discuss whether the children think that these fairy tales have the same moral message as 'Little Red'.

4 Skills focus   See pages 74 to 75

Use the information from the **Skills guide** and the relevant **Skills graphic** to introduce the skill of inference.

1 Model the skill using the **Unit 7 Modelling slides** and the **Modelling inference** guidance on page 74.

2 The children could then attempt the optional **Inference** questions on page 78. This may be in small groups with adult support as needed.

Answers and marking guidance for all questions are included on pages 74 to 75.

5 Where next?

- **Speaking and listening task:** In pairs, the children could think of some sentences that the wolf might say to Little Red and Granny to show how sorry he is. Allow them to practise their sentences and then ask them to perform using vocal expression so they sound like the wolf. Some children may want to take this further and respond to the wolf as if they were Little Red or Granny.

- **Writing task:** Encourage the children to pretend they are the wolf. Using the **Activity** resource on page 79, the children could write a word to describe how the wolf feels at different stages of the story.

Reading list

Class reads
▸ *Little Red Riding Hood Stories Around the World* by Jessica Gunderson
▸ *Little Red: A Howlingly Good Fairy Tale with a Twist* by Lynn Roberts
▸ *Who's Bad and Who's Good, Little Red Riding Hood? A Story about Stranger Danger* by Steve Smallman
▸ *The Wolf's Story* by Toby Forward

Independent reads
▸ *Honestly, Red Riding Hood was Rotten!* by Trisha Speed Shaskan
▸ *Little Red* by Bethan Woollvin
▸ *'Little Red Riding Hood' (Reading with Phonics)* by Clare Fennell
▸ *'The Three Little Pigs'* by Jo Gray (Linked text: Unit 9)

Non-fiction
▸ *The Ways of the Wolf* by Smriti Prasadam-Halls
▸ *Wolves* by James Maclaine (Linked text: Unit 8)

Poetry
▸ *Fairytale Poems* by Clare Bevan
▸ *Revolting Rhymes* by Roald Dahl

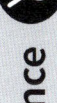

Unit 7 · Inference · Fiction

Modelling inference

☌ **See Unit 7 Modelling slides**

Use the **Skills guide** (see pages 20 to 21) and the downloadable **Skills graphic** to support your modelling.

1 **What did the wolf think when he met Little Red? Tick <u>one</u>.**

   He wanted to run away. ☐

   He wanted to eat Little Red. ☑

   He wanted to use Little Red's skates. ☐

   Emphasise that the answers to inference questions are not found in the text; you need to use clues from the text to work them out. Model reading the question and encourage the children to help you find the key words. Think aloud: *'Think' is one of the key words – it means I need to look not for something the wolf said but for something that tells me what he was thinking.* Ask the children to reread the part of the text where the wolf meets Little Red and look at the possible answers. Continue: *The wolf asked Little Red where her granny lived. After finding this out he 'made a plan'. The text then says that the wolf ran to Granny's house, which shows he wanted to get there before Little Red and put his plan into action. We find out later on that the wolf wanted to eat Little Red – he says, "All the better to eat you with!" – so the answer must be that the wolf wanted to eat Little Red when he met her.* Model ticking one answer only and checking it against the question.

2 **Yes or no? Was Little Red scared of the wolf?**

   no

   Encourage the children to help you find and reread the part of the text where the wolf meets Little Red. Think aloud: *Would Little Red have spoken to the wolf if she was scared? I don't think she would – she would've screamed or run away. However, the text does say that 'the wolf looked scary', so I will read on to check.* Continue: *Here it says '… but Little Red was brave'. This means that she was not afraid to face the wolf, so I don't think she was scared.* Model writing the answer and checking it against the question.

3 **Why did the wolf dress up as Granny?**

   He wanted to trick Little Red into thinking he was Granny.

   Point out that this question starts with 'Why', so the answer needs to include a reason. Encourage the children to reread the part of the text where the wolf dresses up. Think aloud: *The text says that the wolf put on Granny's dress and got into her bed. The wolf knows that Little Red is on her way to Granny's house, so he must be trying to trick her into thinking that he is Granny.* Model writing the answer and checking it against the question.

4 **How do you know that Little Red thought she had done something wrong at the end of the story?**

   Little Red said sorry to her mum.

   Think aloud: *This question asks 'How do you know', which means that we need to find a clue in the text. The question also has a locator: it tells me that I need to look for my answer at the end of the story.* Encourage the children to scan for the clue in the final lines of the text. Continue: *Little Red says sorry to her mum for not listening to her advice about not talking to strangers. People say sorry when they feel they have done something wrong, so this must be the answer.* Model writing the answer and checking it against the question.

Inference questions mark scheme

📖 See page 78

The following guidance can be used with the children if support is needed.

	Answer	Guidance
1	Granny looked different because it was actually the wolf dressed up.	Remind the children that because they are making an inference the answer won't be found in the text; they will need to use clues from the text to work it out. If necessary, support them to find the relevant part of the text, and encourage them to think about what they already know. **Award 1 mark for any reference to the wolf being disguised as Granny.**
2	He would have eaten Little Red. ✓	Support the children to find the relevant part of the text. Encourage them to think about what the woodcutter does in the story and what the wolf was about to do before the woodcutter arrived. Remind them to tick one answer only. **Award 1 mark for the correct answer ticked.**
3	Little Red was in danger. ✓	Remind the children to reread the relevant part of the text and think about how they would react if they were the woodcutter. Encourage them to think about situations in which someone might scream and what they would think if they heard a scream. Remind them to tick one answer only. **Award 1 mark for the correct answer ticked.**
4	The wolf felt scared that the woodcutter would punish him. *OR* The wolf felt guilty.	Encourage the children to use the locator to find the relevant part of the text. Remind them that there should be a clue in the text. You could prompt the children to reread the line: 'The wolf took Little Red's skates and dashed away as quickly as he could'. Encourage them to think about why the wolf wanted to get away so quickly. **Award 1 mark for a plausible feeling.**

Schofield & Sims *Complete Comprehension 1*

Little Red, by Jo Gray

This is the story of Little Red, which is based on the tale of Little Red Riding Hood. Little Red bakes a cake and wants to take it to her granny. Little Red's mum reminds her not to talk to strangers on the way to Granny's house. Do you think Little Red will listen to her mum?

Once upon a time there was a girl called Little Red Riding Hood, or Little Red for short. She lived near a wood with her mum.

One day Little Red made a cake. She wanted to take it to her granny. She put the cake on a plate.

"Can I skate to Granny's?" Little Red asked her mum.

"Yes," said her mum, "but do not talk to strangers."

Little Red put on her skates and her red cape and set off.

On her way, Little Red met a wolf.

"Hello!" said the wolf. "Where are you going?"

"I'm going to see my granny," said Little Red.

The wolf looked scary but Little Red was brave.

"Where does she live?" asked the wolf.

"She lives in a house in the woods," said Little Red.

Then Little Red skated to her granny's house.

The wolf made a plan. He ran through the woods to Granny's house and ate Granny up. He put on Granny's dress and got into Granny's bed.

When Little Red got to the house, Granny looked different.

"Granny, what big eyes you have!" she said.

"All the better to see you with!" said the wolf.

"Granny, what big ears you have!" said Little Red.

"All the better to hear you with!" said the wolf.

"Granny, what big teeth you have!"

"All the better to eat you with!" shouted the wolf.

He jumped out of the bed.

A woodcutter was nearby. He heard a loud scream and ran to the house. The woodcutter chased the wolf and hit him over the head. The wolf screamed and Granny jumped back out.

The wolf took Little Red's skates and dashed away as quickly as he could.

Little Red's mum came to Granny's house.

Little Red said, "I'm sorry, Mum."

At last, Little Red, Granny, Mum and the woodcutter ate the nice cake.

Inference

Name: _____

1 Why do you think Granny looked *different* when Little Red got to Granny's house?

_____

1 mark

2 What do you think the wolf would have done if the woodcutter had not arrived? Tick **one**.

He would have eaten Little Red. ☐

He would have made friends with Little Red. ☐

He would have baked a cake. ☐

1 mark

3 The woodcutter heard Little Red scream and ran to the house. What was the woodcutter thinking? Tick **one**.

Little Red was happy. ☐

Little Red was in danger. ☐

Little Red was having a party. ☐

1 mark

4 How do you think the wolf felt at the end of the story?

_____

1 mark

Activity

Name: _____

Write a word to say how the wolf feels about each event. Use the word bank to help you. Then see if your partner used the same words as you.

When he meets Little Red, the wolf feels

_____.

When he talks to Little Red at Granny's house, the wolf feels

_____.

When he runs away, the wolf feels

_____.

The next day, when he thinks about what he has done, the wolf feels

_____.

Word bank

| scared | angry | sad | guilty | cheeky | playful | hungry | silly | bad |

Wolves

by James Maclaine

▽ **Printable text** • **Modelling slides**   📖 **Photocopiable text and questions** • **pages 84 to 87**

Our first non-fiction text provides a helpful contrast to the Unit 7 text, as it explores the topic of wolves in a real-life context rather than a storybook setting. In reading this information text, the children will become familiar with features of non-fiction texts, such as subheadings. They will also learn facts about wolves: specifically, how they behave in packs compared to how they behave alone. The discussion of baby wolves also provides a link to the Key Stage 1 science curriculum.

❶ Get ready

Discuss the **Key vocabulary** identified in the **Language toolkit** and then complete the vocabulary and phonics activities as desired. Please note that the selected vocabulary is a guide. Depending on the needs of your cohort, additional vocabulary discussion may be beneficial before, during and after reading. Next, display the text (pages 84 to 85) so the children can see the title and any illustrations, and encourage the children to answer the following questions before reading.

1. **This is an information text. What is an information text?**
   It tells you something true/gives you facts about something. Some children may say it is about 'real life'. They may also say that information texts tend to be about a certain topic. Support the children to understand that if a text is based on facts rather than the author's imagination, it is called non-fiction. An information text is a type of non-fiction text.

2. **Looking at the pictures and the Key vocabulary, what kind of information do you think this text will give us?**
   Answers will vary. Most children are likely to simply answer 'wolves', but others may be more specific, using the **Key vocabulary** to think about what facts the text might contain.

3. **Do you think there will be similarities between this text and 'Little Red'?**
   Answers will vary (e.g. *Yes, because both texts mention a wolf; No, because the wolf in 'Little Red' is made up but this text is about real wolves. Real wolves don't wear clothes and they can't talk to humans*).

Language toolkit

Key vocabulary

between	different	family
groups	leaders	lone
mother	usually	wolves

Vocabulary discussion questions

- What other words are there for **mother**?
- Who do you know that is a **leader**?
- Who is in your **family**?

Vocabulary activities

Discuss which sentence makes the most sense.

1. **Wolves** usually live in houses. OR **Wolves** usually live in dens.
2. I sat **between** my **mother** and my father. OR I sat **between** myself.

Phonics

Year 1 phonics	catch, find, hunt, hurt
Split digraphs	female, male, place, same, life, sizes, time, lone
gh	fight, might
Common exception words	are, has, it, she, so, the, there, they
Contractions	can't, doesn't

Phonics activity

Ask the children to correct the sentence below.

th wolf baybies ar born in a den
The children should add a capital letter to the start and a full stop to the end. They should also correct the spelling of 'the', 'babies' and 'are'.

2 First steps

Read the text together and then encourage the children to discuss the following questions.

1. **Point to the place in the text where I can find out about lone wolves.**
   The children may point to the second subheading. This would be a suitable point to discuss that the purpose of subheadings in a non-fiction text is to separate sections of text.

2. **Is this text about one topic or is it about more than one topic?**
   Answers will vary depending on the children's understanding of subheadings. Support them to understand that there is one main topic: wolves, but that the text has three sections that are each about a different topic related to wolves: **Pack life**, **Lone wolf** and **Baby wolves**.

3. **What fact from this text did you find the most interesting?**
   Answers will vary as they will depend on the children's preferences. Some may prefer reading about wolves that fight and others may prefer the information about baby wolves. Emphasise that there is no correct answer. You could point out that not all readers enjoy the same things, which is why discussing texts with others is so interesting.

3 Explore

- Encourage the children to think about the features of non-fiction texts compared to fiction texts. As a class, with you scribing, write down the characteristics of the wolves in this unit's non-fiction text and compare them to the characteristics of the wolf in 'Little Red' (Unit 7) (e.g. in non-fiction texts, wolves often live in packs but sometimes live on their own, don't wear clothes and can't talk to humans; however, fictional texts often feature a lone wolf who wears clothes and can talk to humans).

- You may want to extend the thinking of more able children by asking them why there could be similarities in the two lists, such as appearance, diet and fierce behaviour. Support them to understand that this is because the author will have thought about real wolves when writing 'Little Red'.

4 Skills focus   *See pages 82 to 83*

Use the information from the **Skills guide** and the relevant **Skills graphic** to introduce the skill of retrieval.

1. Model the skill using the **Unit 8 Modelling slides** and the **Modelling retrieval** guidance on page 82.

2. The children could then attempt the optional **Retrieval** questions on page 86. This may be in small groups with adult support as needed.

Answers and marking guidance for all questions are included on pages 82 to 83.

5 Where next?

- **Speaking and listening task:** Provide the children with photographs of wolves in their habitat, or use the illustrations that accompany the text. Ask the children to come up with some words to describe wolves (e.g. brave fighters, gentle with their babies). You could repeat the exercise with an image of the wolf in 'Little Red' (Unit 7).

- **Writing task:** Encourage the children to create a poster that shares facts from the text. This will give them further practice in retrieving information from the text. The children could use the template provided in the **Activity** resource on page 87.

Reading list

Class reads
- *Beware of the Storybook Wolves* by Lauren Child
- *Wolves* by Emily Gravett

Independent reads
- 'Little Red' by Jo Gray (Linked text: Unit 7)
- *National Geographic Kids Readers: Wolves* by Laura Marsh
- 'The Three Little Pigs' by Jo Gray (Linked text: Unit 9)

Non-fiction
- *Face to Face with: Wolves* by Jim and Judy Brandenburg

Poetry
- *The Boy Who Cried Wolf* by Blake Hoena
- *Little Wolf's Handy Book of Poems* by Ian Whybrow

Websites
- National Geographic Kids has a great video about grey wolves on its YouTube channel.

Music
- *Peter and the Wolf* by Sergei Prokofiev (1936). There are many recordings of this famous piece. One of the most popular is narrated by David Bowie (1978).
- "Who's Afraid of the Big Bad Wolf?" by Frank Churchill, from *The Three Little Pigs* (Disney, 1933).

Modelling retrieval

 See Unit 8 Modelling slides

Use the **Skills guide** (see pages 16 to 17) and the downloadable **Skills graphic** to support your modelling.

1 **How many wolves can be found in a pack?**

   between two and twenty

   Emphasise that in retrieval questions, the answer will be found in the text. Model reading the question and highlighting the key words. Think aloud: *This question asks how many wolves can be found in a pack, so I will look under the subheading* **Pack life**, *as it contains the word 'pack'*. Model scanning the text. Continue: *Here it says, 'There can be between two and twenty wolves in a pack'. I will underline this as I think this is the answer*. Model writing the answer and checking it against the question.

2 **Tick one answer to complete the sentence.**

   The pack leaders are often …

   children of the other wolves. ☐

   not related to the other wolves. ☐

   parents of all the other wolves. ☑

   Model reading the question and highlighting the key words. Think aloud: *The question asks me to tick one answer to complete the sentence. The sentence says, 'The pack leaders are often …', so I think this answer will also be found under the subheading* **Pack life**. Model scanning the text for key words from the question. Continue: *Here it says, 'A big male wolf and a big female wolf lead the pack. They are called the pack leaders'. However, this is not one of the possible answers, so I will keep on reading*. Continue: *Here it says, 'They are often the parents of all the other wolves'. This is in the list of possible answers, so I will tick it*. Model ticking one answer only and checking it against the question.

3 **What might happen if a lone male wolf and a lone female wolf meet?**

   They might start a new pack.

   Think aloud: *This question requires me to write an answer. As it is a retrieval question, I know I will be able to find the answer in the text*. Model reading the question and highlighting the key words. *As the question asks what happens if lone wolves meet, I think the answer will be under the subheading* **Lone wolf**. Model locating the subheading and scanning this section for key words from the question. Continue: *Here it says, 'If a lone male wolf and a lone female wolf meet, they might start a new pack'*. Model writing the answer and checking it against the question.

4 **Find and copy one fact about a change that takes place once baby wolves are born.**

   They can't see or hear for a week. Then, they open their eyes and ears.

   Think aloud: *This question asks for one fact from the text. It says 'copy', so I should write the answer exactly as it is in the text. I am looking for a fact about a change that happens once a wolf is born*. Encourage the children to tell you where they might find this information (under **Baby wolves**). Model scanning this section. Think aloud: *I have read two facts that could be the right answer: 'They can't see or hear for a week. Then, they open their eyes and ears' and 'Baby wolves have blue eyes that turn brown, green or orange as they get older'. They are both correct, but the question asks for only one fact*. Model writing one of the answers and checking it against the question.

Retrieval questions mark scheme

See page 86

The following guidance can be used with the children if support is needed.

	Answer	Guidance
1	a big male wolf and a big female wolf	Ask the children to read the question and think about which subheading they need to look under (**Pack life**). Model scanning this section until you come to: 'A big male wolf and a big female wolf lead the pack'. Encourage the children to write the answer and then check it against the question. **Award 1 mark for the correct answer.**
2	different ages and sizes. ✓	Ask the children to read the question and highlight any key words that tell them how to answer (e.g. 'tick one'). Ask them to tell you which subheading they need to look under (**Pack life**). Support them to find the answer in the text and encourage them to check their answer once they have ticked one box. **Award 1 mark for the correct answer ticked.**
3	lone wolves	Encourage the children to think about what it means for a wolf to leave their pack – it means they will be all by themselves. Ask them which subheading they need to look under (**Lone wolf**). Remind them to check that what they have written answers the question. **Award 1 mark for the correct answer.**
4	She picks it up with her mouth. *OR* She holds it very gently so it doesn't get hurt.	Encourage the children to think about which subheading they need to look under (**Baby wolves**). Remind them to choose only one fact for their answer and to check that what they have written answers the question. **Award 1 mark for a correct answer.**

Wolves, by James Maclaine

Most wolves live in the wild, so it is unlikely that you will have seen one near your home! Have you ever seen a wolf on television, or maybe in a zoo? What do you know about wolves? This extract from a non-fiction text will tell you lots of facts about wolves.

Pack life

Wolves live in groups called packs. The wolves in a pack are usually from the same family.

There can be between two and twenty wolves in a pack.

The wolves in each pack are different ages and sizes.

A big male wolf and a big female wolf lead the pack.

They are called the pack leaders. They are often the parents of all the other wolves.

Lone wolf

Many wolves stay in their pack all their lives. Others leave their pack and live on their own. They are called lone wolves.

A lone wolf moves from place to place. Each day it has to find water to drink. It also hunts for food. It eats small animals it can catch on its own.

If a lone male wolf and a lone female wolf meet, they might start a new pack.

Lone wolves try to keep away from wolf packs.

If a lone wolf meets a pack, they might fight.

Baby wolves

A mother wolf has around six babies at a time. Baby wolves are called pups or cubs.

The babies are born in a den. After they are born, the mother licks them clean.

They can't see or hear for a week. Then, they open their eyes and ears.

For the first two months, the baby wolves drink their mother's milk.

If a mother wolf needs to move one of her babies, she picks it up with her mouth.

She holds it very gently, so it doesn't get hurt.

Baby wolves have blue eyes that turn brown, green or orange as they get older.

 **Retrieval** Name: _____

1 Who leads a pack of wolves?

_____

_____   1 mark

2 Tick **one** answer to complete the sentence.

The wolves in each pack are …

from different families. ☐

the same age and size. ☐

different ages and sizes. ☐   1 mark

3 What is the name given to wolves that leave their packs?

_____   1 mark

4 Find and copy **one** fact that explains how a wolf carries her babies.

_____

_____   1 mark

Activity

Name: _____

Design a poster to tell people some facts about wolves. Use the text and the word bank to help you.

Word bank

| lone wolf | leader | cub | pack | den | hunt | fight |

Unit 9

The Three Little Pigs
by Jo Gray

Sequencing • Fiction

▽ Printable text • Modelling slides 📖 Photocopiable text and questions • pages 92 to 95

Like 'Little Red' in Unit 7, this popular fairy tale has been adapted so that young children can apply their phonics to read the text more independently. In this version, the Three Little Pigs respect each other's feelings and work as a team against the wolf – you could discuss their empathetic behaviour with the children. The text's exploration of the best building materials also links well to the science curriculum for this age group.

1 Get ready

Discuss the **Key vocabulary** identified in the **Language toolkit** and then complete the vocabulary and phonics activities as desired. Please note that the selected vocabulary is a guide. Depending on the needs of your cohort, additional vocabulary discussion may be beneficial before, during and after reading. Next, display the text (pages 92 to 93) so the children can see the title and any illustrations, and encourage the children to discuss the following questions before reading.

1. **What type of text is this? How do you know?**
   Answers will vary (e.g. *I think this is a fairy tale because the picture shows three pigs and a wolf*). Support the children to understand that a fairy tale is a type of made-up story and is therefore an example of fiction.

2. **Have you read any stories that are similar?**
   Answers will vary (e.g. *'Little Red Riding Hood' has a wolf in it as well, so I think this might be a similar story*).

3. **Who is in the story?**
   Looking at the picture, I know that there are three pigs and a wolf. If the children already know the story, they may also mention Mummy Pig.

4. **What do you think will happen in this story?**
   I think that the wolf will be mean to the pigs because the wolf wasn't nice in 'Little Red Riding Hood'. If the children have heard the story of 'The Three Little Pigs' then they may retell it.

Language toolkit

Key vocabulary

brother	build	careful
chimney	finished	fire
hasty	kind	knocked

Vocabulary discussion questions

- What materials would you use to **build** a house?
- Would you rather be **hasty** or **careful** when building a house?
- Is **fire** a good thing or a bad thing?

Vocabulary activities

Discuss which sentence makes the most sense.

1. The wolf **knocked** on the **fire**. OR
   The wolf **knocked** on the door.

2. A **fire** is a **chimney**. OR
   A house might have a **chimney**.

Phonics

Year 1 phonics	build, burnt, clever, first, hair, house
Split digraphs	came, made, fire, home, used, time
Common exception words	come, he, his, house, my, no, once, one, there, said, your

Phonics activity

Ask the children to correct the sentence below.

th big bad wolf bernt his bottom

The children should add a capital letter to the start and a full stop to the end. They should also correct the spelling of 'the' and 'burnt'. Some may add capital letters to 'Big Bad Wolf'.

Schofield & Sims Complete Comprehension 1

2 First steps

Read the text together and then encourage the children to discuss the following questions.

1. **What happens at the start of the story?**
   At the start of the story Mummy Pig tells the Three Little Pigs that they need to find their own houses.

2. **What does Pig One/Two/Three do?**
   He builds a house out of straw/sticks/bricks.

3. **What happens at the end of the story?**
   The wolf can't blow down the house made of bricks so he climbs on to the roof and goes down the chimney. The pigs light a fire and the wolf burns his bottom!

4. **What was your favourite part of the story?**
   Answers will vary. The children might choose the part where the pigs build their house, the repetitive refrain '…not by the hair of our chinny-chin-chins!', or the part where the wolf gets his comeuppance.

3 Explore

Draw the children's attention to the repetition of dialogue in the text (e.g. 'let me come in'; 'not by the hair of my chinny-chin-chin'). Allow them to spend a few minutes working in pairs to find these phrases in their copies.

- Encourage the children to work in groups of four to retell the story of 'The Three Little Pigs'. Ask them to focus on the voices and to think about how each character might speak. This will help them to become more aware of the need to use vocal expression when reading aloud.

- You could also explore the relationship between the three brothers. Pig Two and Pig Three do not make fun of their brother for being hasty and building a straw house, and later in the story Pig Three treats his brothers kindly after the wolf has blown down both of their houses. The children could discuss how the three pigs treat each other compared to how they treat the wolf, and why. With regular practice, this skill will become increasingly automatic and will transfer into all their reading.

4 Skills focus   See pages 90 to 91

Use the information from the **Skills guide** and the relevant **Skills graphic** to introduce the skill of sequencing.

1. Model the skill using the **Unit 9 Modelling slides** and the **Modelling sequencing** guidance on page 90.

2. The children could then attempt the optional **Sequencing** questions on page 94. This may be in small groups with adult support as needed.

Answers and marking guidance for all questions are included on pages 90 to 91.

5 Where next?

- **Speaking and listening task:** In pairs, the children could take turns to pretend they are the wolf and talk about what he thinks and how he feels after trying to blow down each of the pigs' houses.

- **Writing task:** Using the text and the **Activity** resource on page 95, the children could write adjectives or whole sentences to describe each character from the story.

Reading list

Class reads
- ▶ *Beware of the Storybook Wolves* by Lauren Child
- ▶ *Inside the Villains* by Clotilde Perrin
- ▶ *The Three Horrid Little Pigs* by Liz Pichon
- ▶ *The Three Little Javelinas* by Susan Lowell
- ▶ *The Three Little Superpigs* by Claire Evans
- ▶ *Three Little Wolves and the Big Bad Pig* by Eugene Trivizas
- ▶ *The Three Ninja Pigs* by Corey Rosen Schwartz
- ▶ *The True Story of the Three Little Pigs* by Jon Scieszka
- ▶ *Where's the Big Bad Wolf?* by Eileen Christelow
- ▶ *Wolves* by Emily Gravett

Independent reads
- ▶ *Three Little Pigs* by Clare Fennell

Non-fiction
- ▶ *Pigs* by Robin Nelson
- ▶ *Wolves* by James Maclaine (Linked text: Unit 8)

Poetry
- ▶ *Fairytale Poems* by Clare Bevan
- ▶ 'The Three Little Pigs' from *Revolting Rhymes* by Roald Dahl (Linked text: Unit 10)

Modelling sequencing

▽ See Unit 9 Modelling slides

Use the **Skills guide** (see pages 18 to 19) and the downloadable **Skills graphic** to support your modelling.

1 **Number the events to show the order in which they happened in the story.**

The wolf blew down the house made out of straw.	2
The pigs had to leave Mummy Pig's home.	1
The wolf blew down the house made out of sticks.	3
The wolf could not blow down the house made of bricks.	4

This may be the first time that the children have answered questions in this format. Explain that first you will need to find the events mentioned in the question in the text. Think aloud: *I will highlight the four events as we find them. Here's the first one: 'One day, she sent them out to find their own homes'. That means that the pigs had to leave Mummy Pig's home. I will highlight this and write a number 1.* Repeat this process with the other three events. You could ask the children to do the same on their own sheets and discuss what they find. Finally, model filling in the answer boxes and then checking them against the question.

2 **What did the wolf do to the other houses before he tried to blow down the brick house?**

He blew them down.

Model reading the question and highlighting the key words. Think aloud: *I need to find out what happened to the other houses before the wolf tried to blow down the brick house. Let's find the part where the wolf visits the first house – that was the straw house, built by Pig One. It says the wolf 'knocked at the door of the straw house', so the answer must be near this part of the text.* Model skim-reading the section. Continue: *Here it says, 'he huffed and he puffed, and he blew the house down'. This will form part of my answer.* Repeat the process for the second house, encouraging the children to contribute to the discussion. Continue: *I know the wolf blew down the house of sticks and the house of straw before he tried the brick house. I need to use this information in my answer.* Model writing the answer and checking it against the question.

3 **What happened after the wolf went down the chimney?**

The wolf burnt his bottom on the fire and ran away.

Think aloud: *I know this happened towards the end of the story, so I don't need to read the whole text again. I will start at the last paragraph. It says, 'When the wolf came down the chimney he landed on the fire and burnt his bottom! The wolf ran away, never to be seen again'. I will use this to write my answer.* Model writing the answer with the children's input and checking it against the question.

4 **Summarise this story using <u>four</u> sentences.**

The three little pigs built houses out of straw, sticks and bricks. The wolf blew down the house made of straw and the house made of sticks. The wolf could not blow down the house made of bricks. He tried to get in through the chimney but burnt himself on the fire.

This question is quite challenging for Year 1 so ask the children to work in pairs to retell the story in their own words first. Next, work together to identify four main events in the story (you may want to highlight them in the text). Think aloud: *I can't rewrite the whole text as I can only write four sentences. The first important part is when each pig builds a house. I will write: 'The three little pigs built houses out of straw, sticks and bricks'.* Repeat with three more key events in the text. Encourage the children to discuss each event with you, and to keep referring back to the text. Finally, model checking your answer against the question.

Sequencing questions mark scheme

📖 See page 94

The following guidance can be used with the children if support is needed.

	Answer	Guidance
1	The pigs built a house each. ✓	Remind the children to find and highlight each of the possible answers in the text. Encourage them to then find the first time the wolf tried to blow down a house and then look back at the highlighted events that come before this to help them select the right answer. Remind them to tick one answer only. **Award 1 mark for the correct answer ticked.**
2	The wolf went down the chimney but the pigs had lit a fire so he burnt his bottom and then he ran away.	Ask the children to find and highlight the relevant part of the text. Encourage them to look at what happens next in the story. Prompt them to write down two things that happen. **Award 1 mark for any reference to the wolf getting cross/ going down the chimney. Award another mark for any reference to the pigs lighting a fire and/or the wolf running away. Do not accept answers that only refer to the wolf hurting himself.**
3	Mummy Pig asked the pigs to find their own homes. ✓	Ask the children to find each event in the text and highlight it. They could then number them in the order in which they happened. If necessary, encourage the children to think about which of the events happened at the very start of the story. Remind them to tick one answer only. **Award 1 mark for the correct answer ticked.**
4	The wolf tried to get the three little pigs. [2] The pigs built their own houses. [1] The pigs lived happily ever after. [4] The wolf ran away. [3]	Ask the children to work in pairs to find, highlight and number the events in the text before filling in the answer boxes. The events take place over several paragraphs, so encourage them to look at the whole text, thinking about what happens at the beginning, middle and end of the story. **Award 1 mark for the correct numbers in at least two boxes.** **Award 2 marks for the correct numbers in all boxes.**

The Three Little Pigs, by Jo Gray

In this story, the Three Little Pigs leave their mummy to build new homes. Do you think they will be safe from the Big Bad Wolf? Will they be safer together or apart?

Once upon a time there was an old mummy pig who had three little pigs. One day, she sent them out to find their own homes.

Pig One felt that straw would be good to build a house with. He used straw to build his home. He finished first but he was hasty.

Pig Two did not think straw would be good to build a house with. He felt that sticks would be best. He used sticks to build his home. He finished second but he was careful.

Pig Three did not think sticks or straw would be good to build a house with. He felt that bricks would be best. He used bricks to build his home. He finished last but he was clever.

Soon the Big Bad Wolf came and knocked at the door of the straw house. He said, "Little pig, little pig, let me come in."

Pig One said, "No, no, no. Not by the hair of my chinny-chin-chin!"

"Then I'll huff and I'll puff, and I'll blow your house down!" said the wolf. So he huffed, and he puffed, and he blew the house down. Pig One ran to his brother's house.

Pig Two was kind to his brother. He did not tell him that straw was no good to build a house with.

The Big Bad Wolf came and knocked at the door of the house made of sticks. He said, "Little pigs, little pigs, let me come in."

Pig One and Pig Two said, "No, no, no. Not by the hair of our chinny-chin-chins!"

"Then I'll huff and I'll puff, and I'll blow your house down!" said the wolf.

So the wolf huffed, and he puffed, and he blew the house down. Pig One and Pig Two ran to their brother's house.

Pig Three was kind to his brothers. He did not tell them that straw and sticks were no good to build a house with.

The Big Bad Wolf came and knocked at the door of the brick house. He said, "Little pigs, little pigs, let me come in."

The Three Little Pigs said, "No, no, no. Not by the hair of our chinny-chin-chins!"

"Then I'll huff and I'll puff, and I'll blow your house down!" said the wolf. So he huffed, and he puffed, and he puffed, and he huffed, but he could not blow the brick house down.

Then the Big Bad Wolf got cross. He told the Three Little Pigs that he would come down the chimney and eat them up.

The Three Little Pigs lit a fire. When the wolf came down the chimney, he landed on the fire and burnt his bottom! The wolf ran away, never to be seen again. The Three Little Pigs felt that bricks were best for building a house with. They lived happily ever after.

Sequencing

Name: _____

1 What happened before the wolf tried to blow down the houses? Tick **one**.

The wolf ate a pig. ☐

The pigs built a house each. ☐

The wolf burnt his bottom. ☐

1 mark

2 What happened after the wolf tried to blow down the house made of bricks?

_____

_____

2 marks

3 Which of these events happened first? Tick **one**.

Pig Two built his house out of sticks. ☐

The wolf blew down the straw house. ☐

Mummy Pig asked the pigs to find their own homes. ☐

1 mark

4 Number the events to show the order in which they happened in the story.

The wolf tried to get the three little pigs. ☐

The pigs built their own houses. ☐

The pigs lived happily ever after. ☐

The wolf ran away. ☐

2 marks

Activity

Name: _____

Write a word or a sentence to describe each character. Use the text and the word bank to help you.

Pig One

_____

_____

_____

Pig Two

_____

_____

_____

Pig Three

_____

_____

_____

Mummy Pig

_____

_____

The Wolf

_____

_____

Word bank

old	kind
hasty	careful
clever	big
bad	cross

Unit 9 — The Three Little Pigs, by Jo Gray

Unit 10 — Inference — Poetry

The Three Little Pigs (Revolting Rhymes)
by Roald Dahl

▽ **Printable text** • **Modelling slides**   📖 **Photocopiable text and questions** • pages 100 to 103

This extract from Roald Dahl's parody of 'The Three Little Pigs' provides an interesting contrast to the more traditional treatment of the same fairy tale in Unit 9. The vocabulary in this poem is at a slightly higher level than the texts so far: however, the children should now have good background knowledge of this story, as well as that of 'Little Red Riding Hood' (see Unit 7). In this text, the third Pig phones Little Red Riding Hood and asks her for advice on how to deal with the Big Bad Wolf. The text provides an excellent opportunity for making comparisons between different versions of traditional tales.

① Get ready

Discuss the **Key vocabulary** identified in the **Language toolkit** and then complete the vocabulary and phonics activities as desired. Please note that the selected vocabulary is a guide. Depending on the needs of your cohort, additional vocabulary discussion may be beneficial before, during and after reading. Next, display the text (pages 100 to 101) so the children can see the title and any illustrations, and encourage the children to discuss the following questions before reading.

1. **What type of text is this? How do you know?**
   Answers will vary. Some children are likely to be able to use the title and illustration to help them identify the text type (e.g. *I think this is a fairy tale because I can see Little Red Riding Hood and one of the Three Little Pigs in the picture*). Some children may also comment on the layout of the text (e.g. *I think this is a poem because of the short lines*). Explain that both answers are correct, as the text is a version of a fairy tale in the form of a poem. You could remind the children that traditional tales often exist in many different versions, linking back to your discussion of 'Little Red' in Unit 7.

2. **Have you read any texts that are similar? How might this text be different?**
   Answers will vary (e.g. *I have read the story of 'Little Red Riding Hood' and I have read the story of 'The Three Little Pigs' but I haven't read a story where all of the characters are together*).

3. **What do you think will happen in this text?**
   Encourage the children to use the illustration to make a prediction (e.g. *Maybe the Pig and Little Red Riding Hood will decide to get the Big Bad Wolf back for being mean; I think Little Red Riding Hood will decide to visit the Three Little Pigs*).

Language toolkit

Key vocabulary

approached	course	creeping
darling	dealt	dialled
dynamite	quietly	telephone

Vocabulary discussion questions

- What is **dynamite** used for?
- Can you do everything **quietly**?
- How have you **dealt** with a problem before?

Vocabulary activities

Discuss which sentence makes the most sense.

1. I **dialled** the number on the **telephone**. OR
   I **dealt** the number on the **telephone**.
2. The wolf **approached** the house. OR
   The house **approached** the wolf.

Phonics

Year 1 phonics	dead, enough, hair, hide, inside, known, mouse, night, sweet
Split digraphs	brute, hide
Common exception words	a, come, house, my, of, one, said, she, so, the, there, to, your

Phonics activity

Ask the children to correct the sentence below.

i wil come when mI hair is dry sed Little Red

The children should add a capital letter to the start and a full stop to the end. They should also correct the spelling of 'will', 'my' and 'said'. More able children may suggest adding speech marks.

2 First steps

Read the text together and then encourage the children to discuss the following questions.

1. **What does the Wolf do at the start of the text?**
   He goes to the Pig's house and he tries to blow it down, but he can't.

2. **What does the Wolf do next? What does the Pig do?**
   The Wolf tells the Pig that he will come back with dynamite to blow the house up. The Pig decides to ring Little Red Riding Hood.

3. **What does the Pig tell Little Red Riding Hood on the phone?**
   He says that he has a wolf at his door and that he knows she has dealt with wolves before.

4. **What does Little Red Riding Hood say to the Pig?**
   She says she will dry her hair and then come and help him.

3 Explore

- The children could practise reciting the poem, working in groups of four (narrator, Wolf, Pig, Little Red Riding Hood). You could help them to mark their parts with a highlighter. Once they feel confident with their parts, encourage them to work on using vocal expression to bring the characters to life. You may wish to give them costumes and/or plastic telephones to help with this. The children could then perform the poem for another class or for their parents. Alternatively, they could record themselves and share the recording on the school website.

- Ask the children whether this text is similar to other fairy tales they know. How is it different? To start the discussion, you could ask them to talk in groups about what they like and what they dislike about this version of 'The Three Little Pigs' compared to other versions they know, including that in Unit 9 if this unit has been completed.

4 Skills focus   See pages 98 to 99

Use the information from the **Skills guide** and the relevant **Skills graphic** to introduce the skill of inference.

1. Model the skill using the **Unit 10 Modelling slides** and the **Modelling inference** guidance on page 98.

2. The children could then attempt the optional **Inference** questions on page 102. This may be in small groups with adult support as needed.

Answers and marking guidance for all questions are included on pages 98 to 99.

5 Where next?

- **Speaking and listening task:** The children could work with a partner to try to make a prediction about what might happen next in the poem. How would they continue the poem?

- **Writing task:** Ask the children to read the poem and look for pairs of words that rhyme. They could write down some of the rhymes they find using the **Activity** resource on page 103.

Reading list

Class reads
- *The Atlas of Fairy Tales* by Claudia Bordin
- *The Deep Dark Wood* by Algy Craig Hall
- *The Great Fairy Tale Disaster* by David Conway
- *Into the Forest* by Anthony Browne
- *Little Red Reading Hood* by Lucy Rowland
- *The Once Upon a Time Map Book* by B. G. Hennessy
- *The Stinky Cheese Man and Other Fairly Stupid Tales* by Jon Scieszka
- *Who's Afraid of the Big Bad Book?* by Lauren Child

Independent reads
- 'Little Red' by Jo Gray (Unit 7)
- *Mixed Up Fairy Tales* by Hilary Robinson
- National Geographic Kids Readers: *Wolves* by Laura Marsh
- 'The Three Little Pigs' by Jo Gray (Linked text: Unit 9)

Non-fiction
- *Exploring the World of Wolves* by Tracy C. Read

Poetry
- *Fairytale Poems* by Clare Bevan

 **Modelling inference** ▽ See Unit 10 Modelling slides

Use the **Skills guide** (see pages 20 to 21) and the downloadable **Skills graphic** to support your modelling.

1 **How can you tell that the Wolf doesn't give up easily?**

   The Wolf doesn't give up easily because when he can't blow down the Pig's house, he says he will come back with dynamite.

   Model reading the question and highlighting the key words. Explain that 'How can you tell' is another way of saying 'How do you know'. Discuss what it means to not 'give up easily' (be determined to get what you want). Remind the children that, as this is an inference question, you will need to use clues from the text. Model skim-reading the first three verses to look for clues about the Wolf's behaviour. Think aloud: *The text says the Wolf will come back at night and use dynamite to blow the house up. This means he doesn't give up when he can't blow the house down straight away – he makes another plan.* Model writing the answer with the children's input and checking it against the question.

2 **Why do you think the Pig decides to ring Little Red Riding Hood?**

   The Pig knows that she escaped from a wolf and he thinks she might be able to help him.

   Encourage the children to tell you which character Little Red Riding Hood and the Three Little Pigs both escape from (the Wolf). Think aloud: *I think the Pig has read 'Little Red Riding Hood' – or perhaps he is her friend, as he has her telephone number. He obviously knows her story.* Continue: *I think the Pig knows that the Wolf tried to eat Little Red Riding Hood but she escaped. The Pig must be thinking that she can help him escape too.* Next, ask the children to help you to find evidence that supports this idea. Find the line, 'I know you've dealt with wolves before' and explain that this supports your idea. Finally, model writing the answer with the children's input and checking it against the question.

3 *He dialled as quickly as he could/the number for Red Riding Hood.* **Why does the Pig dial the number quickly? Tick <u>one</u>.**

He doesn't want to forget the number.	☐
He needs a wee.	☐
He is scared that the wolf will come back.	✓

   Encourage the children to use the locator to help you find the relevant part of the text, and highlight it. Think aloud: *The Pig dials the number quickly because he is in a rush, but why is he in a rush?* Model looking at the possible answers and reading the text before and after the target sentence. Continue: *The Wolf says he will come back to blow up the Pig's house; if you were the Pig, how would that make you feel?* Encourage the children to suggest feelings such as 'worried' or 'scared' and model using these to help you select your answer. Model ticking one answer only and checking it against the question.

4 **True or false? Little Red Riding Hood is in a rush to help the Pig. Circle <u>one</u>. Explain your answer.**

   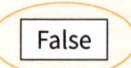

   She decides to wait for her hair to dry first!

   Discuss the meaning of 'true' and 'false'. Encourage the children to identify and highlight the key words. Think aloud: *I wonder if I can find any clues that suggest that Little Red Riding Hood is in a rush.* Model scanning the last two verses and explain that you can't find anything that supports this idea. Continue: *Little Red Riding Hood says, "I've just begun to wash my hair/But when it's dry, I'll be right there". That, to me, means she isn't in a rush, because if she was in a rush she would have left her hair wet and gone to help the Pig straightaway.* Model circling 'False', writing an explanation with the children's input and checking it against the question.

Inference questions mark scheme

📖 See page 102

The following guidance can be used with the children if support is needed.

	Answer	Guidance
1	She isn't sure who is on the phone at first. ✓	Encourage the children to find the relevant part of the text. Ask them to pretend to answer the phone themselves, saying, "Who's speaking? Who?" Ask them to think about why Little Red Riding Hood asks 'Who?' twice. Explore situations in which you might ask a caller to repeat their name (e.g. if you didn't recognise the voice of the caller or if you couldn't hear them very well). Remind the children to tick one answer only. **Award 1 mark for the correct answer ticked.**
2	(False)	Discuss the meaning of 'true' and 'false'. Then ask the children to find the relevant part of the text. Support them to notice that 'The house stayed up as good as new' after the Wolf tried to blow it down, which suggests that it is strong. Encourage them to tell you that the statement in the question is false. More able children may want to write down why. Remind the children to circle one answer only. **Award 1 mark for the correct answer circled.**
3	He needs to get the dynamite first. ✓	Support the children to find the relevant part of the text. Ask them if they can tell you how the Wolf's plan changes when he can't blow down the Pig's house (he decides to blow the house up with dynamite instead). Prompt them to think about whether the Wolf has the dynamite with him (no, because he was expecting to blow the house down with his breath). Support them to notice that if he already had the dynamite with him, he would have used it straightaway. Remind the children to tick one answer only. **Award 1 mark for the correct answer ticked.**
4	The Wolf does not want the Pig to hear that he is there/he wants to surprise the Pig and eat him!	Support the children to find the relevant part of the text. Ask them what it means to 'creep'. Discuss why the Wolf is being so quiet and ask the children to think about what the Wolf wants to do (blow the house up/eat the Pig) and what would happen if the Pig heard the Wolf (the Pig might run away or get help). **Award 1 mark for any reference to the Wolf not wanting the Pig to hear him.**

Schofield & Sims Complete Comprehension 1

The Three Little Pigs (Revolting Rhymes), by Roald Dahl

This text is from a poem based on the story of the Three Little Pigs. The poem was written by Roald Dahl and is a different version of the traditional story. The poem also includes the character Little Red Riding Hood. Now that they are in the same story, do you think that the Three Little Pigs and Little Red Riding Hood will be on the same side? The text begins when the Wolf arrives at the brick house and tries to blow it down.

So creeping quietly as a mouse,
The Wolf approached another house,
A house which also had inside
A little piggy trying to hide.

"You'll not get me!" the Piggy cried.
"I'll blow you down!" the Wolf replied.
"You'll need," Pig said, "a lot of puff,
And I don't think you've got enough."
Wolf huffed and puffed and blew and blew.
The house stayed up as good as new.

"If I can't blow it down," Wolf said,
"I'll have to blow it up instead.
I'll come back in the dead of night
And blow it up with dynamite!"
Pig cried, "You brute! I might have known!"
Then, picking up the telephone,
He dialled as quickly as he could
The number of Red Riding Hood.

"Hello," she said. "Who's speaking? Who?
Oh, hello, Piggy, how d'you do?"
Pig cried, "I need your help, Miss Hood!
Oh help me, please! D'you think you could?"
"I'll try, of course," Miss Hood replied.
"What's on your mind ...?" "A Wolf!" Pig cried.
"I know you've dealt with wolves before,
And now I've got one at my door!"

"My darling Pig," she said, "My sweet,
That's something really up my street.
I've just begun to wash my hair.
But when it's dry, I'll be right there."

From *Revolting Rhymes* by Roald Dahl, copyright ©1982 Roald Dahl. Published by Puffin Books.

Inference

Name: _____

1 Why does Little Red Riding Hood say *"Who's speaking? Who?"* when she answers the phone? Tick **one**.

- She isn't sure who is on the phone at first. ☐
- She is eating ice cream. ☐
- The Wolf is at her door. ☐

1 mark

2 True or false? The Pig's house is not very strong. Circle **one**.

| True | False |

1 mark

3 Why does the Wolf say he will come back to blow up the house? Tick **one**.

- He likes visiting the Pig. ☐
- He needs to get the dynamite first. ☐
- He wants to go home for his tea first. ☐

1 mark

4 Why does the Wolf creep as *quietly as a mouse* towards the Pig's house?

_____
_____

1 mark

Activity

Name: _____

How many rhyming words can you find in the poem? Write them in pairs. One has been done for you.

__mouse__ rhymes with __house__

_____ rhymes with _____

_____ rhymes with _____

_____ rhymes with _____

_____ rhymes with _____

_____ rhymes with _____

_____ rhymes with _____

_____ rhymes with _____

Unit 10

The Three Little Pigs (Revolting Rhymes), by Roald Dahl

Unit 11

Looking After Rabbits
by Fiona Patchett

▽ Printable text • Modelling slides   📖 Photocopiable text and questions • pages 108 to 111

This non-fiction text is about caring for a pet – a subject that most children will be able to relate to, as many have or want pets. The text is perfect for improving the children's knowledge of features of information texts such as suggestion boxes and subheadings, and each section is short enough to keep the children engaged. You could use this text to make links to the topic of animal habitats in the Key Stage 1 science curriculum.

1 Get ready

Discuss the **Key vocabulary** identified in the **Language toolkit** and then complete the vocabulary and phonics activities as desired. Please note that the selected vocabulary is a guide. Depending on the needs of your cohort, additional vocabulary discussion may be beneficial before, during and after reading. Next, display the text (pages 108 to 109) so the children can see the title and any illustrations, and encourage the children to discuss the following questions before reading.

1   **This text is an information text. What is an information text?**
    An information text tells you facts about a topic. The children may also be able to explain that an information text is a type of non-fiction text. You could remind them of your discussions of the text in Unit 8 if this unit has been completed.

2   **What types of information text have you read before?**
    The children may refer to books that they have read at home or independently, or to topics they have learnt about in class. Some children may refer to the information text in Unit 8.

3   **Do you enjoy reading non-fiction texts? Why?**
    This will depend on the reading preferences of the individual: some children enjoy reading anything and everything; others only like fiction or non-fiction. You could use this as an opportunity to point out that every reader has different reading habits and that this is what makes reading so exciting – there is something for everyone.

4   **Do you have any pets? What pet would you most like to have?**
    Answers will vary. Some children may not have any experience of pets; others may be involved in caring for multiple pets. To boost background knowledge, you could discuss how the children with pets help to look after them.

Language toolkit

Key vocabulary

chemicals	grazing	minerals
nibbles	occasional	pellets
variety	vegetables	vitamins

Vocabulary discussion questions

- Which foods should you only eat **occasionally**?
- Which foods contain **vitamins** and **minerals**?
- Why might there be harmful **chemicals** on **vegetables**? How could you remove them?

Vocabulary activities

Discuss which sentence makes the most sense.

1   The house was **grazing** on grass. *OR*
    The sheep was **grazing** on grass.

2   **Pellets** are dried-up food for animals. *OR*
    Pellets are toys for animals.

Phonics

Year 1 phonics	feed, food, good, need
Split digraphs	make, take, like, use
ea	clean, each, eat, leave, treat
Common exception words	and, are, of, put, the, they, you, your
–ing/–ed suffix	chopped, eating, hiding, preparing, mixing, grazing

Phonics activity

Ask the children to correct the sentence below.

yur rabbits ned to eyt fresh vegetables evry day

The children should add a capital letter to the start and a full stop to the end. They should also correct the spellings of 'your', 'need' and 'eat'. Some may also correct the spelling of 'every'.

2 First steps

Read the text together and then encourage the children to discuss the following questions.

1. **Can you point to the first subheading? What does it tell us?**
   The first subheading is 'Dry food'. It tells us that we are going to read about the dry food that rabbits can eat. Depending on your cohort, and on whether Unit 8 has been completed, the children may need to be reminded of the purpose of subheadings.

2. **What did you learn from this text?**
   Answers will vary, and may be general (e.g. *I learnt about what rabbits can eat*) or more specific (e.g. *I learnt that rabbits can be fussy about what they eat*).

3. **Now that you have read the text, do you think that caring for a rabbit would be easy or tricky?**
   Answers will vary. Some children may refer to a specific piece of information that makes them think looking after a rabbit would be tricky (e.g. 'only give them a few teaspoons of pellets, or they'll get fat'), or they may answer more generally (e.g. *It would be tricky because there is so much to remember*). Others may feel that it is easy to care for a rabbit, especially if they have one at home.

3 Explore

- Use the text to discuss some features of non-fiction texts (e.g. title, subheadings, topic-related vocabulary, illustrations and 'Try this!' boxes). Which features can the children name and which are new to them? You may find it helpful to display some additional non-fiction texts from this book, such as Unit 8 or Unit 15, to help the children familiarise themselves with these features. You could also use books from the class library to draw the children's attention to whole-book features (e.g. contents page; other types of illustration such as diagrams and photographs; glossary; index).

- Explain that it is a good idea to scan for the key words when reading a non-fiction text to learn about a new topic. Working in small groups on an assigned subheading, the children could practise this skill by underlining the key words in their section of the text. For further scanning practice, you could ask the children to scan the text for 'food and drink' words. How many can they find? You could challenge them to divide the words into foods just for rabbits and foods that both people and rabbits can eat.

4 Skills focus   See pages 106 to 107

Use the information from the **Skills guide** and the relevant **Skills graphic** to introduce the skill of word meaning.

1. Model the skill using the **Unit 11 Modelling slides** and the **Modelling word meaning** guidance on page 106.

2. The children could then attempt the optional **Word meaning** questions on page 110. This may be in small groups with adult support as needed.

Answers and marking guidance for all questions are included on pages 106 to 107.

5 Where next?

- **Speaking and listening task:** In pairs, the children could take on the roles of a pet-shop owner and a customer who wants a pet rabbit. The customer should ask questions and the pet-shop owner should answer based on facts from the text (e.g. Customer: *Can I feed my rabbits chocolate as a treat?* Pet-shop owner: *No, it will make them poorly.* Customer: *How about lettuce?*). The children could then swap roles and repeat the exercise.

- **Writing task:** Using the text and the **Activity** resource on page 111, the children could write a fact beside each picture. Emphasise that they should use information from the text rather than their own ideas.

Reading list

Class reads
- *Secret Life of Pets: Junior Novel* by Centum Books

Independent reads
- *Amazing Animals* by Guinness World Records
- *Axel Scheffler's Flip Flap Pets* by Axel Scheffler
- *I want a Pet* by Lauren Child

Non-fiction
- *How to Look After Your Pet Rabbit* by David Alderton
- *Little Kids First Big Book of Pets* by Marfe Ferguson-Delano (ed)

Poetry
- 'The Pet' by Tony Bradman, from *Dragon Poems* by John Foster (ed) (Linked text: Unit 12)
- *Pet Poems* by Jennifer Curry

Films
- *The Secret Lives of Pets* (Universal, 2016)
- *The Secret Lives of Pets 2* (Universal, 2019)

Websites
- The CBBC website has a useful fact sheet called 'How to – look after rabbits'.

Modelling word meaning

See Unit 11 Modelling slides

Use the **Skills guide** (see pages 14 to 15) and the downloadable **Skills graphic** to support your modelling.

1. **Look at the first two sentences. Which word tells you that rabbits need a mixture of foods? Circle one.**

     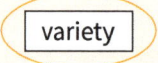

   Model reading the question and highlighting the key words. Think aloud: *This question has a locator, so I know I need to look at the first two sentences to find my answers.* Model rereading the sentences and continue: *All the possible answers are in this part of the text. What do I already know?* Discuss the meaning of each word in turn: *'Dry' means 'waterless' or 'not wet'. 'Hay' means 'dried grass'. Neither of these words means 'a mixture'.* Continue: *'Variety' is the only other possible answer. 'Mixture' and 'variety' have similar meanings, so 'variety' must be the correct word.* Model circling one answer only and checking it against the question.

2. **The text tells us that rabbits chew on hay all day. Find and copy one word that means the same as 'chew'.**

   munch

   Think aloud: *This question asks me to find one word and copy it from the text.* Model rereading the question. Continue: *The word I'm looking for needs to mean the same as 'chew'. 'Hay' is another key word – I have seen a subheading called Hay, so I will look there.* Model scanning for the subheading and then rereading the section. Think aloud: *It says, 'Rabbits like to munch on hay all through the day'. This must be the right section. 'Munch' could be the word we need.* Ask the children to see if they can identify any other words that are similar to 'chew'. Continue: *I can't find another word that is similar to 'chew', so I think the answer must be 'munch'.* Model writing the answer and checking it against the question.

3. **Draw lines to match the words to their meanings.**

   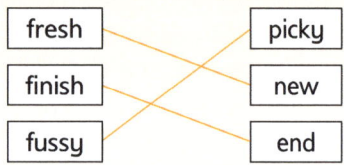

   Ask the children to help you find the words from the left-hand column in the text and highlight them (note that 'fresh' is used several times). Then ask them to read the sentences containing these words. Think aloud: *First, I will read a sentence with the word 'fresh' in it – 'fill it with fresh water every day'.* Discuss that 'fresh' must mean 'new'. Repeat for the other two words. Model matching up the answers and checking them against the question. When you have finished, model checking that the lines you have drawn are clear.

4. **What does the word *pellets* mean?**

   dry food (for rabbits)

   Model finding and highlighting the word 'pellets' in the text. Ask: *What subheading is this under?* (**Dry food**). Read the sentence that contains the word 'pellets': *'Pellets are the best dry food'.* You may also want to show the children a picture of rabbit pellets to help them to understand this. Model writing the answer and checking it against the question.

Word meaning questions mark scheme

📖 See page 110

The following guidance can be used with the children if support is needed.

	Answer	Guidance
1	occasional	Support the children to use the locator to find the relevant subheading. Ask them if they know the meaning of any of the possible answers ('fresh' and 'pellets' were both discussed in the **Modelling questions**). Encourage them to highlight 'fresh', 'occasional' and 'pellets' in the text and to identify which word is under the subheading mentioned in the question. If necessary, direct them to the sentence: 'Fruit is okay as an occasional treat'. Remind them to tick one answer only. **Award 1 mark for the correct answer ticked.**
2	hutch	Remind the children that this question asks them to copy one word only from the text. Ask them to scan for a word that they know means the same as 'cage'. If necessary, prompt them to reread the sections **Hay** and **Water**. **Award 1 mark for the correct answer.**
3	treat — cut chopped — luxury (crossed: treat—luxury, chopped—cut) dirty — unclean	Remind the children that they first need to find the words in the left-hand column in the text. They should then reread the sentences that contain these words and think about which of the words in the right-hand column would make sense in their place. Finally, support them to draw clear lines to show their answers. **Award 1 mark for one pair correctly matched. Award 2 marks for all pairs correctly matched.**
4	uncooked/not cooked	Support the children to find the word 'raw' in the text by prompting them to reread the section **What to give**. Read the relevant sentence together and discuss what it means. Ask them if they have ever eaten raw carrot before. How does it differ from carrot they might have as part of a hot meal? **Award 1 mark for the correct answer.**

Looking After Rabbits, by Fiona Patchett

Do you know how to care for a rabbit? What do they need to eat and what are they not allowed to eat? This extract from a non-fiction information text will help you find out more.

Rabbit food

Rabbits need a variety of dry food, fresh food and lots of hay. Feed them dry food in the morning and fresh food later on.

Dry food

Pellets are the best dry food, because they have all the vitamins and minerals that rabbits need. If you feed your rabbits pieces of dried fruit and vegetables, they'll only pick out the ones they like best and leave the rest.

How much?

When your rabbits are young, put plenty of food in their dish each morning. They will eat as much as they need.

When your rabbits are six months old, only give them a few teaspoons of pellets, or they'll get fat.

Rabbits should finish their pellets in about an hour. The rest of the day is spent grazing on fresh food and hay.

Hay

Hay is dried grass. Rabbits like to munch on hay all through the day, so make sure there's always plenty in your rabbits' hutch.

Try this!

Treasure hunt

In the wild, rabbits have to search for tasty nibbles, so pet rabbits enjoy doing the same. Try hiding chopped carrots around their run and let your rabbits sniff them out.

Water

Rabbits need lots of water, especially when the weather is hot. Bowls of water can get dirty in a hutch, so use a water bottle. Remember to fill it with fresh water every day.

Fresh food

Your rabbits need to eat fresh vegetables every day to stay fit and healthy.

What to give

They like eating raw vegetables such as carrots, broccoli, cauliflower and celery. Lettuce is no good, because it gives them an upset stomach. Fruit is okay as an occasional treat.

What not to give

Rabbits should only eat vegetables, fruit, hay and grass. Anything else could be bad for them.

Preparing fresh food

Wash the vegetables to get rid of any chemicals. Carefully cut them into chunky pieces. Put fresh food in your rabbits' dishes in the afternoon or early evening.

When you clean out the hutch before bed, take away anything that hasn't been eaten. Food that starts to go bad can make your rabbit very sick.

Try this!

Mixing it up

Rabbits are fussy eaters and it takes them time to get used to new food. The best way to get them eating something new is to mix it with food they already like.

From *Looking after Rabbits* by Fiona Patchett, copyright © 2013 Usborne Publishing Ltd. Reproduced by permission of Usborne Publishing, 83–85 Saffron Hill, London, EC1N 8RT, UK. www.usborne.com.

Word meaning

Name: _____

1 Look at the subheading **What to give**. Which word tells you that rabbits should only have fruit every now and then? Tick **one**.

fresh ☐

occasional ☐

pellets ☐

1 mark

2 Find and copy **one** word that means the same as 'rabbit's cage'.

_____

1 mark

3 Draw lines to match the words to their meanings.

treat		cut
chopped		luxury
dirty		unclean

2 marks

4 The author uses the word *raw*. What does it mean?

_____

1 mark

Activity

Name: _____

Write a fact to go with each picture. Use the text to help you.

Hay

_____

_____

Water

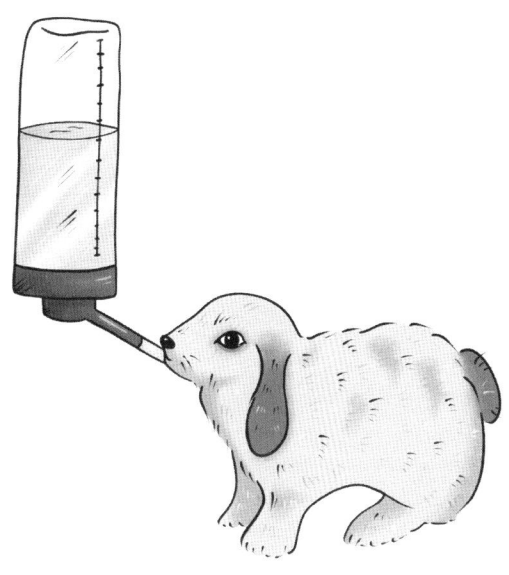

_____

_____

Fresh food

_____

_____

Fruit

_____

_____

The Pet
by Tony Bradman

Unit 12 · Prediction · Poetry

▽ **Printable text** · **Modelling slides** · 📖 **Photocopiable text and questions** · **pages 116 to 119**

'The Pet' is a great poem to use with Year 1 as the children will already be familiar with the topic, both from everyday life and from their discussions in Unit 11. However, this time there is a twist: the child in the poem chooses a dragon as his pet! This unit provides opportunities for introducing the children to descriptive language as well as encouraging them to make predictions based on evidence from the text.

❶ Get ready

Discuss the **Key vocabulary** identified in the **Language toolkit** and then complete the vocabulary and phonics activities as desired. Please note that the selected vocabulary is a guide. Depending on the needs of your cohort, additional vocabulary discussion may be beneficial before, during and after reading. Next, display the text (pages 116 to 117) so the children can see the title and any illustrations, and encourage the children to answer the following questions before reading.

1. **What is a poem and how is it different from other types of text?**
   Discuss the children's answers and support them to expand on them. Explain that in a poem, the words are carefully chosen by a poet to help tell a story or explain a feeling, theme or idea. Poems have rhythm and play with sound. Some poems rhyme, but others do not.

2. **Have you read or heard any other poems?**
   You could discuss nursery rhymes as a type of poem (see Units 3 and 4) or refer to the extract from 'The Three Little Pigs' in Unit 10.

3. **If you could have any animal as a pet, what would you choose? Why?**
   Answers will vary. Encourage the children to think about unusual pets (e.g. *a unicorn, because they are magical; a monkey, because they are funny; a turtle, so we can have a pool for them to swim in*).

4. **Have you read any texts that might be similar?**
   The children may refer to other texts about pets (e.g. *Looking After Rabbits* from Unit 11) or to other stories about dragons (see the **Reading list** for some examples).

5. **What do you think will happen in this poem?**
   Encourage the children to structure their answers with "I think … because …" (e.g. *I think the poem is about someone's pet because it is called 'The Pet'*).

Language toolkit

Key vocabulary

burning	desire	gleaming
money	orange	shiny
wandered	window	wonder

Vocabulary discussion questions

- What could you buy with lots of **money**?
- Can you think of anything that is **gleaming** and **shiny**?
- What would be dangerous if it was **burning**?

Vocabulary activities

Discuss which sentence makes the most sense.

1. The child had a **desire** to **window**. OR
   The child had a **desire** to own a pet.

2. I **wandered** through the town. OR
   I **wonder** through the town.

Phonics

Year 1 phonics	clouds, flash, round, tail, treat
Split digraphs	flame, gave, made, scales, desire, fire, home, hope
Common exception words	a, he, I, is, me, my, of, said, she, so, some, the, to

Phonics activity

Ask the children to correct the sentence below.

i gayv the man sum mony

The children should add a capital letter to the start and a full stop to the end. They should also correct the spelling of 'gave'. More able children may correct 'some' and 'money'.

112 · Schofield & Sims Complete Comprehension 1

2 First steps

Read the text together and then encourage the children to discuss the following questions.

1. **What does the child get at the start of the poem?**
   They are given some money to buy a treat.

2. **What does the child do next?**
   They go to the shops to choose what to buy.

3. **How does the child know what to spend their money on?**
   The child sees a pet shop and sees something they want in the window/sees a dragon. Some children may also refer to the child knowing what not to buy (e.g. *They know they are not allowed to buy any sweets*).

3 Explore

- Discuss which parts of the poem the children find amusing. They will most likely enjoy the description of the pet – although it doesn't say it explicitly, the poem implies that the child has bought a dragon! Encourage the children to help you look for hints from the poem that suggest this.

- Point out that the poem is separated into verses and discuss why this is (e.g. to make it easier for the reader to read; to identify the different parts of the poem's story; to build up the clues that tell us what sort of pet the child chooses).

- Talk about why the poet has used a rhyme in each verse (e.g. because it makes the poem catchy and easy to remember; it gives the poem a rhythm).

- The children could practise performing the poem to strengthen their recitation skills. They could learn the whole poem individually or they could each learn a different part of the poem and then put it all together to recite it.

4 Skills focus   See pages 114 to 115

Use the information from the **Skills guide** and the relevant **Skills graphic** to introduce the skill of prediction.

1. Model the skill using the **Unit 12 Modelling slides** and the **Modelling prediction** guidance on page 114.

2. The children could then attempt the optional **Prediction** questions on page 118. This may be in small groups with adult support as needed.

Answers and marking guidance for all questions are included on pages 114 to 115.

5 Where next?

- **Speaking and listening task:** Ask the children to reread the poem and identify the words that rhyme. Once they have identified the rhyming words, they can write down more words that rhyme with those in the poem (e.g. treat, sweets, meat, beat, cheat).

- **Writing task:** The children could imagine that they have been given money to treat themselves and are allowed to go to the shops – what would they buy? What if there was a pet shop – what would they choose? Would they need to buy anything to help them look after their new pet? They could discuss their ideas with a partner and then write them down using the **Activity** resource on page 119.

Reading list

Class reads
- *The Boy who Grew Dragons* by Andy Shepherd
- *Dare to Care: Pet Dragon* by Sally Symes and Mark Robertson
- *The Funny Life of Pets* by James Campbell
- *A World Full of Animal Stories* by Angela McAllister

Independent reads
- *Dragon Post* by Emma Yarlett
- *Dragon Stew* by Steve Smallman
- *The Great Pet Sale* by Mick Inkpen
- *How to Catch a Dragon* by Caryl Hart
- *There is No Dragon in this Story* by Lou Carter
- *There's a Dragon in Your Book* by Tom Fletcher

Non-fiction
- *An Anthology of Intriguing Animals* by Ben Hoare
- *Atlas of Animal Adventures* by Rachel Williams and Emily Hawkins
- *Dragonology: The Complete Book of Dragons* by Dugald Steer
- *Looking after Rabbits* by Fiona Patchett (Linked text: Unit 11)
- *Unusual Pets* by Pat Jacobs

Poetry
- *Dragon Poems* by John Foster (ed)
- *Evidence of Dragons* by Pie Corbett
- *Pet Poems* by Jennifer Curry

Modelling prediction

▽ See Unit 12 Modelling slides

Use the **Skills guide** (see pages 22 to 23) and the downloadable **Skills graphic** to support your modelling.

1   **When did you realise what sort of pet the child had chosen?**
    I realised that the child has chosen a dragon when it said 'a flash of fire', 'scales' and 'a pet with wings'.

    Think aloud: *To answer this question we need to find the part of the poem where we first realise the pet is a dragon. If we read the text carefully, the first clue is where it says, 'There in a pet shop window/I saw a flash of fire'.* Ask the children to identify some more clues. Continue: *If I keep on reading I find 'scales', 'burning eyes' and 'wings'. Now I need to write all this as an answer.* Encourage the children to discuss how they would do this. Model writing an answer and checking it against the question.

2   **How do you think the child's mum will feel when they bring their pet home? Why?**
    I think she will be unhappy because the dragon breathes fire and is a dangerous creature.

    Think aloud: *First of all I need to think about what I know about dragons and then imagine what my mum would say if I took a dragon home. I have to use what I already know, as the answer won't be given in the text. I'm making a guess, or a prediction.* Encourage the children to discuss their ideas and then continue: *I don't think my mum would be happy.* Encourage the children to think about why Mum would not be happy. *Not many people have dragons as pets, probably because they are so big. They also breathe fire, which I think is brilliant, but I think my mum would say it is dangerous.* Discuss how the phrase 'I hope that it's OK' shows that the child suspects that their mum will not be happy with their new pet. Model writing an answer with the children's input and checking it against the question.

3   **What do you think will happen to the dragon?**
    I think the child will have to take it back to the pet shop because it will be too big for the house.

    Think aloud: *This question asks me what I think, so I need to imagine what would happen if I took a dragon home.* Continue: *I know dragons are big, so a pet dragon might not fit into my house. The child also says that the dragon's tail is 'longer than any tail you've seen', so it must be huge. I know that my mum wouldn't like the dragon's fire-breathing, so she might not allow it inside. I couldn't just leave the dragon outside though – it might feel lonely – so I would probably have to return it to the shop.* Model writing an answer with the children's input and checking it against the question.

4   **Which of these do you think the child will not say if their mum tells them to take the pet back? Tick one.**

    "That's fine, Mum."   ✓
    "But it can live under the stairs."   ☐
    "That's not fair."   ☐
    "You said I could buy anything as long as it wasn't sweets."   ☐

    Point out that 'not' is underlined in this question. Think aloud: *I know the answer is not in the text so I need to make a sensible guess or prediction. We have already discussed what the child's mum would say about the dragon. The child really likes the dragon – how will they feel?* Continue: *Let's look at the choices. Which one would you definitely not say to your mum if she told you to take back something you really wanted to keep?* Model ticking the answer and checking it against the question.

Prediction questions mark scheme

📖 See page 118

The following guidance can be used with the children if support is needed.

	Answer	Guidance
1	"We cannot have a dragon for a pet!" ✓	Remind the children of your discussion about how the child's mum would feel about a pet dragon. Remind them that their answer needs to be a sensible guess or prediction based on the text. Remind them not to choose the option that they would like the child's mum to say, but the one they think she would be most likely to say. **Award 1 mark for the correct answer ticked.**
2	I think the child's mum will say that they aren't allowed to buy sweets or a pet. OR She might go with the child to the shops to make sure they don't buy anything they shouldn't.	Explain to the children that their answer should be a prediction or a guess. Encourage them to think about the things their parents or caregivers do to make sure they stick to the rules at home. **Award 1 mark for a plausible prediction.**
3	No – I don't think the child would know how to look after a dragon because it is an unusual pet/because the child has never had a pet dragon before. OR Yes – because the pet-shop owner might have told the child how to look after the dragon.	Remind the children of the need to make a sensible prediction. Encourage them to think about whether the child is likely to have looked after a dragon before: would they know what a dragon likes to eat, how often it needs a walk or how much sleep it needs? Remind them that the question asks them to explain their answer. **Award 1 mark for a plausible prediction. Accept both positive and negative predictions as long as they are linked to the text.**
4	Yes – because the child likes dragons. OR No – because the child's house will be too small.	Discuss the need to make a sensible prediction. Remind the children that the question asks them to explain their answer. **Award 1 mark for a plausible prediction. Accept both positive and negative predictions as long as they are linked to the text.**

The Pet, by Tony Bradman

If your mum gave you some money to treat yourself, what would you buy? What about if you were able to buy a pet? This is a poem about a child who buys a very unusual pet. What sort of pet do you think the child might buy?

My mum gave me some money
To buy myself a treat;
She said I could buy anything
(So long as it wasn't sweets).

So off I went to spend it.
I wandered round the shops,
I couldn't find a thing to buy …
Then something made me stop.

There in a pet shop window
I saw a flash of fire;
I saw some scales and burning eyes
And I knew my heart's desire.

I gave the man my money.
He handed me a lead.
Then I walked out of the pet shop
With the only pet I need.

A pet with wings and gleaming fangs,
With skin that's shiny green;
With claws, and a tail that's longer
Than any tail you've seen.

A pet whose breath is orange flame,
Whose ears both hiss with steam,
Who'll fly me to the land of clouds
And to the land of dreams.

But first I'd better go home.
I hope that it's OK ...
I hope my mum will like my pet.
I wonder what she'll say?

Prediction

Name: _____

1 Which of these do you think the child's mum will say? Tick **one**.

"You can keep the dragon." ☐

"Shall we get a second dragon?" ☐

"A dragon – how lovely." ☐

"We cannot have a dragon for a pet!" ☐

1 mark

2 What do you think the child's mum will do next time they are allowed to buy a treat?

_____

_____

1 mark

3 Do you think the child would know how to look after a dragon? Explain your answer.

_____

_____

1 mark

4 Do you think the dragon would be happy living with the child? Explain your answer.

_____

_____

1 mark

Activity

Name: _____

If you were given some money to buy a treat, what would you buy? Write a shopping list.

My Shopping List

_____

_____

_____

_____

_____

_____

_____

Unit 12 — The Pet, by Tony Bradman

Chocolate Cake

by Michael Rosen

▽ **Printable text** • **Modelling slides**   📖 **Photocopiable text and questions** • **pages 124 to 127**

The text is an extract from the poem 'Chocolate Cake', which was originally published in 1985 but has timeless appeal. It is an ideal poem to use with Year 1 because of its familiar subject matter – who doesn't love cake? The accessible topic should increase the children's ability to engage with the expressive language and poetic form of the text. Written from a young child's point of view, this text is also great fun to read aloud.

1 Get ready

Discuss the **Key vocabulary** identified in the **Language toolkit** and then complete the vocabulary and phonics activities as desired. Please note that the selected vocabulary is a guide. Depending on the needs of your cohort, additional vocabulary discussion may be beneficial before, during and after reading. Next, display the text (pages 124 to 125) so the children can see the title and any illustrations, and encourage the children to answer the following questions before reading.

1 **What type of text is this? How is it different from other types of text?**
   Answers will vary (e.g. *It is a poem. A poem is written a bit like a story but might look or sound like a song. Poems often have short lines and sometimes have rhyming words*).

2 **Have you read any other poems?**
   Answers will vary depending on the children's exposure to poetry. Some children may refer to nursery rhymes as a type of poem (see Units 3 and 4). Others might talk about 'The Three Little Pigs' (Unit 10) or 'The Pet' (Unit 12), if these units have been completed.

3 **When did you last eat chocolate cake? What did you think of it?**
   Answers will vary (e.g. *at a birthday party/at home/it was delicious/gorgeous/yummy/too sweet*).

4 **Have you read anything similar?**
   Answers will vary. The children may refer to stories such as *Charlie and the Chocolate Factory* by Roald Dahl, because it is about chocolate; the traditional fairy tale 'Hansel and Gretel', because it includes sweets and treats; or the poem 'Twinkle Twinkle Chocolate Bar'.

5 **What do you think will happen in this poem?**
   Encourage the children to structure their answers with "I think … because …" (e.g. *I think the boy will eat a chocolate cake because of the title and the picture*).

Language toolkit

Key vocabulary

careful	chocolate	creaky
crept	crumbly	downstairs
kitchen	nibble	treading

Vocabulary discussion questions

- Can you think of any foods that are **crumbly**?
- When have you needed to be **careful**?
- Have you ever **crept** somewhere? Why?

Vocabulary activities

Discuss which sentence makes more sense.

1 He sat **treading** about cake. *OR* He looked where he was **treading** as it was slippery.

2 The stairs were very **creaky**. *OR* The cake was very **creaky**.

Phonics

Year 1 phonics	bare, crumbs, first, scoop
Split digraphs	cake, chocolate, late, plate, take, knife, nice, side, while, woke
Common exception words	once, put, the, so, there, we, your

Phonics activity

Ask the children to correct the sentence below.

i like chocolate cayk because it is delicious

The children should add a capital letter to the start and a full stop to the end. They should also correct the spelling of the split digraph in 'cake'.

2 First steps

Read the text together and then encourage the children to discuss the following questions.

1. Where was the boy at the beginning of the poem?
   He was in bed.
2. Why does the boy wake up?
   He wakes up because he can't stop thinking about the chocolate cake he had for tea.
3. What does the boy do next?
   He goes downstairs to 'nibble' the crumbs of the cake.

3 Explore

- Perform the text in groups. Invent some actions with the children (e.g. licking lips and smiling, scooping up crumbs, treading on toys) and/or ask them to join in with the sound effects (e.g. 'yowwww', 'shhhhhhh', 'ooooooooommmmmmmmm').

- Discuss which parts of the poem the children find amusing. You could talk about how the sound effects make the poem sound funny when it is read aloud. They also help to emphasise certain points in the poem.

- Discuss how this poem is different from other poems the children have read (e.g. *It has very short lines and it does not rhyme, although it does use repetition and sound effects*). Discuss why it might have been written like this (e.g. *It could be to show that a young child is telling the story of what happened – it sounds like the boy is talking to a friend, and makes the character seem more real*). You could also talk about how use of non-standard English (e.g. 'Yeah' and 'proper') also communicates the character's voice in the poem.

4 Skills focus   See pages 122 to 123

Use the information from the **Skills guide** and the relevant **Skills graphic** to introduce the skill of inference.

1. Model the skill using the **Unit 13 Modelling slides** and the **Modelling inference** guidance on page 122.
2. The children could then attempt the optional **Inference** questions on page 126. This may be in small groups with adult support as needed.

Answers and marking guidance for all questions are included on pages 122 to 123.

5 Where next?

- **Speaking and listening task:** The children could reread the text and make predictions about what will happen after the end of the extract. You could then read the poem in its entirety (see the **Reading list**). In pairs, the children could then discuss whether their predictions were correct.

- **Writing task:** Allow the children to keep their copy of the text nearby. Encourage them to imagine they are the boy in the poem and to write about the chocolate cake from his point of view, using the text and the **Activity** resource on page 127. Picture books might be useful inspiration for this activity (see the **Reading list**). You could also refer back to your discussion of senses in Unit 2. If you are feeling generous, you could even supply them with some chocolate cake of their own!

Reading list

Class reads
- *Charlie and the Chocolate Factory* by Roald Dahl
- *The Great Chocoplot* by Chris Callaghan
- 'Hansel and Gretel', traditional fairy tale
- *Lulu and the Chocolate Wedding* by Posy Simmonds

Independent reads
- *Chocolate Mousse for Greedy Goose* by Julia Donaldson
- *Daisy and the Trouble with Chocolate* by Kes Gray
- *I Really Want the Cake* by Simon Philip
- *Mr Bunny's Chocolate Factory* by Elys Dolan
- *Who Ate the Cake?* by Kate Leake

Non-fiction
- *The Best Ever Baking Book* by Jane Bull
- *Chocolate* by Liz Gogerly
- 'Chocolate Cake Recipe' by Jo Gray (Linked text: Unit 14)
- *Make It: Chocolate* by Madison Spielman
- *Smart About: Chocolate* by Sandra Markle

Poetry
- 'Chocolate Cake' from *Quick, Let's Get Out of Here* by Michael Rosen
- *Michael Rosen's A to Z: The best children's poetry from Agard to Zephaniah* by Michael Rosen
- *Twinkle Twinkle Chocolate Bar* by John Foster

Websites
- Michael Rosen's YouTube channel features an enjoyable video of the poet reading 'Chocolate Cake'.

Modelling inference

See Unit 13 Modelling slides

Use the **Skills guide** (see pages 20 to 21) and the downloadable **Skills graphic** to support your modelling.

1 Why do you think the boy decided to go downstairs? Tick **one**.

   to get a drink of water ☐
   to eat some cake
   to find somewhere else to sleep ☐

   Remind the children that, as this is an inference question, they need to look for clues in the text. Think aloud: *This question starts with 'Why do you think', which means it wants me to explain my thoughts.* Model finding the relevant part of the text by scanning for the key word 'downstairs' and rereading the lines immediately before and after it. Continue: *The poem says the boy woke up 'licking [his] lips and smiling' and he could 'almost see' the cake. I think this is why he decided to go downstairs – he wanted to eat the cake!* Model ticking one answer only and checking it against the question.

2 How do you know that the boy was trying to be very quiet?

   I know this because he 'crept' out of his door.

   Think aloud: *This question starts with 'How do you know', so I need to find some clues from the text to back up my answer.* Encourage the children to find the correct part of the text and ask them to discuss it. Continue: *The text says 'crept' and I know that is another word for 'tiptoed'. If he wasn't trying to be quiet, he wouldn't have crept – he would have walked normally. It also says, 'careful not to tread on … Lego' and describes the noise he might make if he did. This makes me think the boy was trying to be quiet.*

3 Why do you think the boy didn't want to wake anybody up?

   He didn't want to wake anybody up because he knew he shouldn't be out of bed.

   Think aloud: *I know that everyone else in the poem was in bed. I know this is an inference question, so I need to use clues from the text to help me.* This question relies on an understanding that children shouldn't be up late at night or when their parents are in bed. Ask: *What would happen if you did this at home?* Continue: *If I was out of bed when I wasn't supposed to be, I would try to be really quiet so no-one knew I was awake.* Model writing an answer with the children's input and checking it against the question.

4 True or false? The boy thought it was nearly the morning. Circle **one**. Explain your answer.

   (False)

   The boy knew it was the middle of the night because it was dark and everyone was in bed.

   If necessary, discuss the meaning of 'true' and 'false'. Encourage the children to look for clues in the text. If necessary, model finding and rereading the lines: 'It was all dark/everyone was in bed/so it must have been really late'. Think aloud: *The boy says it is really late, so he can't think it is nearly morning. The answer must be false.* Model circling 'false' before writing an answer and checking it against the question.

Inference questions mark scheme

See page 126

The following guidance can be used with the children if support is needed.

	Answer	Guidance
1	He couldn't stop thinking about the cake. ✓	Remind the children of their discussion of the **Modelling inference** questions. Encourage them to use the word 'proper' to help them find and highlight the relevant part of the text. Prompt them also to think about the subject of the poem and to look carefully at the possible answers. **Award 1 mark for the correct answer ticked.**
2	The boy is worried about creaky floorboards because they are noisy and might wake his family up.	Remind the children to first find the relevant part of the text. Encourage them to think about what the boy is trying to do (get downstairs without waking anybody up) and then ask them to think about why the boy might mention a creaky floorboard. **Award 1 mark for any reference to waking his family.**
3	No – he plans to (only) eat a little bit of cake/a little nibble/some crumbs.	Explain that the question wording 'Explain your answer' means that the children should refer to a clue from the text in their answer. Encourage them to look for places in the text where the boy mentions eating the cake. **Award 1 mark for any reference to having a small amount/little nibble, eating some crumbs or just tidying up the cake.**
4	(False) The boy wants to avoid treading on the toys with his bare feet and making a noise.	Discuss the meaning of 'true' and 'false'. Encourage the children to scan for the word 'toys' in the text. Then ask them what the boy is trying to do (get downstairs without waking his family). You could ask them if the text talks about playing with toys (no) and discuss what it says about toys (that it hurts if you stand on toys with bare feet). If the children's explanations rely only on the toys being 'broken', refocus them on the boy's reason for being out of bed. Remind them to circle one answer before writing the reason why. **Award 1 mark for the correct answer circled and any reference to avoiding stepping on toys/making a noise.**

Chocolate Cake, by Michael Rosen

What is your favourite kind of cake? The boy in this poem extract loves chocolate cake. One night, he wakes up thinking about the cake he had for tea. He decides to sneak downstairs in the middle of the night to look at it …

Once we had this chocolate cake for tea
and later I went to bed
but while I was in bed
I found myself waking up
licking my lips
and smiling.
I woke up proper.
'The chocolate cake.'
It was the first thing
I thought of.
I could almost see it
so I thought,
what if I go downstairs
and have a little nibble, yeah?
It was all dark
everyone was in bed
so it must have been really late
but I got out of bed,
crept out of the door

there's always a creaky floorboard, isn't there?

Past Mum and Dad's room,
careful not to tread on bits of broken toys or bits of Lego
you know what it's like treading on Lego
with your bare feet,

yowwww
shhhhhhh

downstairs
into the kitchen
open the cupboard
and there it is
all shining.

So I take it out of the cupboard
put it on the table
and I see that
there's a few crumbs lying about on the plate,
so I lick my finger and run my finger all over the crumbs
scooping them up
and put them into my mouth.

Oooooooommmmmmmmm

nice.

Then
I look again
and on one side where it's been cut,
it's all crumbly.
So I take a knife
I think I'll just tidy that up a bit,
cut off the crumbly bits
scoop them all up
and into the mouth

oooooommm mmmm
nice.

Look at the cake again.

From 'Chocolate Cake', from *Quick, Let's Get Out of Here* by Michael Rosen, published by Puffin Books (2017). Copyright © Michael Rosen 1983. Reproduced by permission of Penguin Books Ltd, 80 Strand, London, WC2R ORL.

Inference

Name: _____

1 Why did the boy wake up *proper*? Tick **one**.

He had a tummy ache. ☐

It was morning. ☐

He couldn't stop thinking about the cake. ☐

1 mark

2 *... there's always a creaky floorboard, isn't there?*
How does the boy feel about creaky floorboards?

_____

_____

1 mark

3 Does the boy plan to eat a lot of the cake? Explain your answer.

_____

1 mark

4 True or false? The boy mentions toys because he wants to play with them. Circle **one**. Explain your answer.

☐ True   ☐ False

_____

_____

1 mark

Activity

Name: _____

Imagine you are the boy in the poem. Write words or sentences to describe the chocolate cake. Use the text to help you.

The chocolate cake tasted _____

_____

The chocolate cake smelt _____

_____

The chocolate cake looked _____

_____

The chocolate cake felt _____

_____

Unit 13

Chocolate Cake, by Michael Rosen

Unit 14 — Sequencing — Non-fiction

Chocolate Cake Recipe
by Jo Gray

▽ **Printable text** • **Modelling slides**   📖 **Photocopiable text and questions** • pages 132 to 135

This text uses the familiar topic of baking to introduce the children to a new form of non-fiction: instructional writing. The text has been written in the form of command sentences to help the children begin to understand the use of imperative verbs in written instructions.

❶ Get ready

Discuss the **Key vocabulary** identified in the **Language toolkit** and then complete the vocabulary and phonics activities as desired. Please note that the selected vocabulary is a guide. Depending on the needs of your cohort, additional vocabulary discussion may be beneficial before, during and after reading. Next, display the text (pages 132 to 133) so the children can see the title and any illustrations, and encourage the children to discuss the following questions before reading.

1. **This text is a recipe. What is a recipe?**
   A recipe tells us how to cook something. Support the children to understand that a recipe is a type of non-fiction text that includes a set of instructions to follow to help us cook or bake. You could use the subheadings within this text to discuss the features of recipe texts (e.g. lists of ingredients and equipment followed by a method).

2. **Have you ever followed a recipe before? What were you making?**
   The children's answers will vary depending on their experiences. If necessary, remind them of any experiences that they may have had in school.

3. **What things should you always remember to do when following a recipe?**
   Answers will vary. Encourage the children to come up with several suggestions (e.g. ensure you have the right ingredients and equipment before you start; wash your hands; follow the method in the correct order; be careful not to over- or undercook the food).

Language toolkit

Key vocabulary

equipment	ingredients	measuring
method	mixture	recipe
repeat	sieve	spread

Vocabulary discussion questions

- What steps are there in the **method** for making a cake?
- What **ingredients** might you **sieve** to get rid of lumps?
- Have you ever spent time **measuring** something?

Vocabulary activities

Discuss which sentence makes the most sense.

1. The children followed the **recipe** carefully. *OR* The children baked the **recipe** book.
2. The child asked the teacher to **repeat** the pencil. *OR* The child asked the teacher to **repeat** the question.

Phonics

Year 1 phonics	bowl, flour, fork, oven, smooth, spread, turn, whisk
–er	butter, caster, other, paper, powder, together
Common exception words	ask, once, put, the, to, your

Phonics activity

Ask the children to correct the sentence below.

Line to cayk tins with bayking payper
The children should add a full stop to the end. They should also correct the spelling of 'cake', 'baking' and 'paper'. Some may correct 'two'.

2 First steps

Read the text together and then encourage the children to discuss the following questions.

1. There are two lists at the start of the recipe. What do these tell us?
   The first one tells us what ingredients we need and the second one tells us what equipment we need.

2. What is on the next page of the recipe? What does it tell us?
   The method. It tells us what we need to do/the steps we need to follow to make the cake.

3. Does the recipe give us any other information?
   There are two boxes: one reminds us to wash our hands and one warns us that the oven is hot so an adult should put the cakes in the oven.

3 Explore

- The best way to explore this text would be to allow the children to follow the recipe and make a cake. This will give them experience of baking, while helping them to understand the importance of following instructions carefully.

- Draw attention to the imperative verbs – or 'bossy words' – at the beginning of each instruction in the method (e.g. 'Ask', 'Use', 'Add', 'Repeat'). Have a look at some other examples of recipes (see the **Reading list** for some suggestions) and encourage the children to scan these for more imperative verbs.

- Divide the group into pairs. Give one child in each pair a picture of an elaborately decorated cake and give the other child a plain outline of a cake of the same shape without any decoration. The first child should keep their picture hidden and use imperative verbs and details from the picture to tell their partner how to decorate their plain cake so that the two cakes match.

- You could use the measurements in the text to make links to the maths curriculum, for example by showing the children a full bag of flour and allowing them to compare the weight to a bag containing the 225g needed for the recipe.

4 Skills focus   See pages 130 to 131

Use the information from the **Skills guide** and the relevant **Skills graphic** to introduce the skill of sequencing.

1. Model the skill using the **Unit 14 Modelling slides** and the **Modelling sequencing** guidance on page 130.

2. The children could then attempt the optional **Sequencing** questions on page 134. This may be in small groups with adult support as needed.

Answers and marking guidance for all questions are included on pages 130 to 131.

5 Where next?

- **Speaking and listening task:** In pairs, the children take turns using imperative verbs/'bossy words' to instruct each other to move around the classroom from a given starting point to a given end point, or to complete a task such as building a model, drawing a picture or playing a game (e.g. *Pick up a piece of paper; draw a circle in the middle …*).

- **Writing task:** Using the **Activity** resource on page 135, the children could write an instruction underneath each picture. Each sentence should begin with an imperative verb (e.g. *Cut the paper*).

Reading list

Class reads

▷ *The Chocolate Tree: A Mayan Folktale* by Linda Lowery and Richard Keep

▷ *Ellie's Magical Bakery: Best Cake for a Best Friend* by Ellie Simmonds

Independent reads

▷ *Cake* by Sue Hendra and Paul Linnet
▷ *Daisy and the Trouble with Chocolate* by Kes Gray
▷ *I Really Want the Cake* by Simon Philip
▷ *Who Ate the Cake?* by Kate Leake

Non-fiction

▷ *The Best Ever Baking Book* by Jane Bull
▷ *Children's Book of Baking Cakes* by Abigail Wheatley
▷ *Gruffalo Crumble and Other Recipes* by Julia Donaldson
▷ *Nadiya's Bake Me a Story* by Nadiya Hussain

Poetry

▷ 'Chocolate Cake' from *Quick, Let's Get Out of Here* by Michael Rosen (Linked text: Unit 13)

Websites

▷ The CBeebies 'I Can Cook' website contains a collection of recipes and songs that are suitable for young children.

Modelling sequencing

See Unit 14 Modelling slides

Use the **Skills guide** (see pages 18 to 19) and the downloadable **Skills graphic** to support your modelling.

1. **Number the instructions to show the order in which they appear in the text.**

    Crack the eggs into a bowl and whisk.   1
    Spread one cake with the filling.   4
    Add the baking powder.   3
    Sieve in the self-raising flour.   2

    Explain that, as this is a sequencing question, you need to write numbers in the boxes to show where the instructions come in the recipe. Think aloud: *The numbers I write will not match those found in the text next to each instruction, because my numbers are to put the instructions that are in this question in order to match the text.* Model finding and highlighting the four sentences. Continue: *Now I have found all four instructions in the text, I need to work out which one comes first. I can see that 'Crack the eggs into a bowl and whisk' is first, so that will be number 1.* Repeat for the other statements. Finally, model filling in the answer boxes and checking them against the question.

2. **Which of these instructions is given first? Tick one.**

    The icing sugar is sieved. ☐
    The mixture is spooned into the tins. ☐
    The tins are lined with baking paper. ✓

    Think aloud: *The question is asking me to work out which instruction happened before the others in the list.* Explain that, as in the last question, you need to find the three events in the text. Model scanning for the events in the text and highlighting them. Continue: *I can see that 'Use baking paper to line the cake tins' is similar to 'The tins are lined with baking paper' so I will highlight this.* When you have found all three, model looking at where they appear in the text. Continue: *'The tins are lined with baking paper' comes first so this must be the answer.* Model ticking the answer and checking it against the question.

3. **What instruction is given after the cake mixture has been spooned into the tins?**

    Ask an adult to put the tins into the oven.

    Remind the children that this is a sequencing question and ask them which words in the question are important. Think aloud: *This question uses the word 'after', so it wants me to find the instruction that follows the mixture being spooned into the tins. First, I need to find the instruction that mentions this.* Model scanning the text and then continue: *Instruction 9 says, 'Spoon half the mixture into one cake tin and half into the other cake tin', so the answer must be the instruction after this one.* Model finding the answer, writing it and checking it against the question.

4. **Where in the recipe is the list of ingredients found? Tick one.**

    at the start ✓
    in the middle ☐
    at the end ☐

    Think aloud: *Where have we seen the word 'ingredients' before?* Encourage the children to tell you that there are subheadings in the text and **Ingredients** is one of these. Think aloud: *Where exactly does it say 'ingredients' in the recipe?* Model scanning for the word. When you find it, ask the children where it comes in the recipe – at the start, the middle or the end? Model ticking the answer and checking it against the question.

Sequencing questions mark scheme

See page 134

The following guidance can be used with the children if support is needed.

	Answer		Guidance
1	Mix with the milk to make the filling.	3	You may find it helpful to refer back to **Modelling question 1**. Remind the children that the numbers they write will not match those in the text but will show the order of the instructions. Support them to find, highlight and number the four instructions in the text and work out which one comes first, second, third and fourth. **Award 1 mark for the correct numbers in at least two boxes.** **Award 2 marks for the correct numbers in all boxes.**
	Use baking paper to line the cake tins.	1	
	Blend together until the mixture is smooth.	2	
	Spread one cake with the filling.	4	
2	Ask an adult to turn on the oven. ✓		Explain to the children that the question is asking them to work out which instruction happened before the others in the list. Encourage them to find, highlight and number all three instructions in the text and to tick the one that happens before the other two. **Award 1 mark for the correct answer ticked.**
3	Sieve in the self-raising flour.		Support the children to find the word 'after' in the question. Explain that this means that they need to find the instruction that follows the one in the question. If necessary, support them to find Instruction 4 in the method and write down the instruction that comes next. **Award 1 mark for the correct answer.**
4	after the ingredients ✓		Remind the children of the structure of a recipe and encourage them to scan the text for the word 'Method'. **Award 1 mark for the correct answer ticked.**

Schofield & Sims Complete Comprehension 1

Chocolate Cake Recipe, by Jo Gray

Have you ever baked a cake? Who have you baked with and did you follow any instructions? This is a recipe for a delicious chocolate cake. If you decide to have a go at baking it, make sure you ask an adult to help you.

Ingredients

For the cake:

4 eggs

caster sugar (225g)

butter (225g)

self-raising flour (225g)

cocoa powder (50g)

baking powder (2tsp)

For the filling:

icing sugar (300g)

cocoa powder (50g)

milk (40ml)

Equipment

oven (180°C)

baking paper

2 cake tins (20cm)

3 bowls

whisk or fork

measuring jug and spoons

scales

sieve

Remember

Wash your hands before you start!

Method

1. Ask an adult to turn on the oven.
2. Use baking paper to line the cake tins.
3. Crack the eggs into a bowl and whisk.
4. Put the caster sugar and the butter into a bowl and blend.
5. Sieve in the self-raising flour.
6. Repeat with 50 grams of cocoa powder.
7. Add the baking powder.
8. Blend together until the mixture is smooth.
9. Spoon half the mixture into one cake tin and half into the other cake tin.
10. Ask an adult to put the tins into the oven. The cakes need to cook for 25 to 30 minutes before they come out.
11. Sieve the icing sugar and 50 grams of cocoa powder into a bowl.
12. Mix with the milk to make the filling.
13. Take the cakes out of the tins once they have cooled.
14. Spread one cake with the filling.
15. Put the other cake on top and dust with icing sugar to serve.

Warning

The oven is hot. Make sure you ask an adult to help you put the cakes into the oven and take them out.

Sequencing

Name: _____

1 Number the instructions to show the order in which they appear in the text.

Mix with the milk to make the filling. ☐

Use baking paper to line the cake tins. ☐

Blend together until the mixture is smooth. ☐

Spread one cake with the filling. ☐

2 marks

2 Which of these instructions is given first? Tick **one**.

Sieve in the self-raising flour. ☐

Ask an adult to turn on the oven. ☐

Take the cakes out of the tins once they have cooled. ☐

1 mark

3 What do you do after you have blended the sugar and butter with the eggs?

_____

1 mark

4 Where is the method found in the recipe? Tick **one**.

before the title ☐

after the ingredients ☐

before the ingredients ☐

1 mark

Activity

Name: _____

Write an instruction under each picture. One has been done for you.

Cut the paper.

_____

_____

_____

Plant Facts

by Izzi Howell

▽ Printable text • Modelling slides   📖 Photocopiable text and questions • pages 140 to 143

Many children are intrigued by the plants, flowers and trees they see around them every day and will ask about how they grow. This information text, which responds to that natural curiosity, can be used to make links to the Key Stage 1 science curriculum. As it contains some technical vocabulary, it is worth allocating extra time to vocabulary discussion here. This is the first unit that includes mixed skill questions. For guidance on introducing this new activity, see page 10.

① Get ready

Discuss the **Key vocabulary** identified in the **Language toolkit** and then complete the vocabulary and phonics activities as desired. Please note that the selected vocabulary is a guide. Depending on the needs of your cohort, additional vocabulary discussion may be beneficial before, during and after reading. Next, display the text (pages 140 to 141) so the children can see the title and any illustrations, and encourage the children to answer the following questions before reading.

1. **What sort of text do you think this is?**
   This is an information text. An information text is usually about a topic, and looking at the pictures I think this text may be about plants. You could encourage the children to draw upon knowledge gained from the previous non-fiction units in this book (see Units 8, 11 and 14).

2. **Looking at the pictures and the Key vocabulary, what kind of information do you think this text will give us?**
   I think this text will tell us facts about plants such as how they grow and the different types of plant that we can find. The children may refer to the subheadings in the text if they have completed the previous non-fiction units.

3. **What do you know about plants already?**
   If necessary, remind the children of experiences that they may have had in school. You could also prompt them to think about where and when they have seen plants before and whether they can name any plants that humans eat or use.

4. **Look at the labels on the pictures. Do you know the meaning of any of these words?**
   Encourage the children to articulate their ideas based on details from the pictures. You could also show them images of other plants mentioned in the text (e.g. algae, seaweed, ferns). The Woodland Trust website is a helpful resource for images.

Language toolkit

Key vocabulary

algae	habitat	microscope
nutrients	reproduce	roots
shoot	sprouts	stem

Vocabulary discussion questions

- What types of **habitat** do humans live in?
- What **nutrients** do plants need?
- Why would you need a **microscope**?

Vocabulary activities

Discuss which sentence makes the most sense.

1. Plants can live without the correct **nutrients**. OR Plants cannot live without the correct **nutrients**.
2. I looked at the plant using a **microscope**. OR I looked at the **microscope** using a plant.

Phonics

Year 1 phonics	breaks, found, ground, leaves, tiny
Split digraphs	make, place, concrete, like, sizes, stone
Common exception words	are, come, is, one, so, some, the, there, they, to

Phonics activity

Ask the children to correct the sentence below.

Plants com in meny sizs, from tall trees two tiny algae

The children should add a full stop to the end. Many will also correct the spelling of 'come', 'many' and 'sizes'. Some may also correct 'two' to 'to'.

2 First steps

Read the text together and then encourage the children to discuss the following questions.

1. [Point to the subheadings.] What are these called? What are they for?
   They are called subheadings. They break the text into shorter parts and tell us what we can find out by reading that section. Depending on your cohort, and on whether the previous non-fiction units have been completed, the children may need to be reminded of the purpose of subheadings.

2. What information do the boxes give us?
   They give us extra facts.

3. Which plants are so small that they can only be seen under a microscope?
   (Some types of) algae.

4. What kind of plants grow in the rainforest?
   (Brightly coloured) flowers.

5. Where in the text can we read about leaves?
   Leaves are a part of a plant so I think it will be under the subheading 'Parts of a plant'.

3 Explore

- If possible, take the children to a nearby wood, park or playing field and encourage them to look at the plants that grow there. Challenge them to use the vocabulary from this unit to point out the different parts of a plant. The children could record the types of plant they find or use magnifying glasses to observe the parts of the plants more closely.

- If it is not possible to take the children outside, you may want to look at some different types and parts of plants in the classroom (e.g. pot plant, soil, cactus, seaweed, flower, leaves, stem, bulb).

4 Skills focus   See pages 138 to 139

Use the information from the **Skills guide** and the relevant **Skills graphic** to introduce the skill of word meaning.

1. Model the skill using the **Unit 15 Modelling slides** and the **Modelling word meaning** guidance on page 138.

2. The children could then attempt the optional **Word meaning** questions on page 142. This may be in small groups with adult support as needed.

3. Finally, the optional **Mix it up!** questions on page 143 offer practice in a range of comprehension skills. For guidance on introducing this new activity, see page 10.

Answers and marking guidance for all questions are included on pages 138 to 139.

5 Where next?

- **Speaking and listening task:** Increase the children's background knowledge and strengthen their grasp of the vocabulary from this unit by encouraging them to plant seeds and observe what happens. Discuss the changes they notice every few days. You could use this as an opportunity to model further scientific vocabulary (e.g. germinate, shoot, sprout, etc.). Alternatively, you could use a video clip of a plant growing from seed to encourage the children to discuss the different stages of growth.

- **Writing task:** Following on from the activity above, the children could keep a written record of observations of the plants they have grown or watched in the video clip. Encourage them to draw the plant and label it using some of the **Key vocabulary** from this unit.

Reading list

Class reads
- *A Seed In Need* by Sam Godwin
- *Eddie's Garden and How to Make Things Grow* by Sarah Garland
- *Jody's Beans* by Malachy Doyle

Independent reads
- 'Jack and the Beanstalk' by Jo Gray (Linked text: Unit 16)
- *Plants* by Kathryn Williams
- *Seed to Plant* by Kristin Baird Rattini

Non-fiction
- *100 Facts: Plant Life* by Camilla de la Bedoyere
- *Botanicum* by Kathy Willis
- *How Do Plants Grow?* by Kay Barnham
- *RHS The Magic and Mystery of Trees* by Jen Green
- *Ten Thousand Poisonous Plants in the World* by Paul Rockett
- *Trees, Leaves, Flowers and Seeds* by DK

Poetry
- *A Year of Nature Poems* by Joseph Coelho
- *I Am the Seed That Grew the Tree* by Fiona Waters

Websites
- The KS1 Plants area of the BBC Bitesize website contains learning guides and videos.
- The Woodland Trust website is full of information about plants and wildlife.

Modelling word meaning

See Unit 15 Modelling slides

Use the **Skills guide** (see pages 14 to 15) and the downloadable **Skills graphic** to support your modelling.

1 **Look at the section 'What are plants?'. Find and copy <u>one</u> word that means the same as 'alive'.**

   living

   Think aloud: *I need to copy one word that means 'alive' from the text. The question has a locator, **What are plants?**, so I will look there.* Model scanning for and rereading the section. Continue: *It says 'plants are living things', and 'living' means the same as 'alive'. I'll read on to see if there are any other words.* Continue: *There are no other words that mean 'alive', so the answer is 'living'.* Model writing and checking the answer.

2 **Look at the section 'Plant habitats'. What does the word *habitat* mean?**

   a place where something lives or grows

   Think aloud: *The question asks me to explain what 'habitat' means. It also gives me a locator.* Model scanning for and rereading the section. Continue: *It says, 'Plants grow in many habitats'. I'll read on to see if I can find out more. Here it mentions four different habitats – 'desert'; 'rainforest'; 'seas and oceans'; and 'woodland'. What is the same about all three?* Encourage the children to tell you that they are all places where plants grow. Model writing and checking the answer.

3 **Draw lines to match the words to their meanings.**

   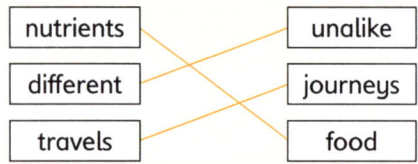

   Think aloud: *First I need to find the words in the left-hand column in the text.* Model scanning for and rereading the relevant sentences. Continue: *First, I'll read the sentence with 'nutrients' in it: 'Plant roots take in water and nutrients from the soil'.* Discuss the words in the right-hand column and explain that 'nutrients' must mean food for plants. Repeat for the other two words. Model matching up and checking the answers.

4 **Under the last subheading, which word describes how roots and a shoot grow from a seed?**

   sprouts

   Model using the locator to find the relevant section. Think aloud: *I need to find the sentence about roots and shoots starting to grow. Here it says: '… its hard shell breaks open and it sprouts roots and a shoot'. This must be the correct sentence. I need to find a word similar to 'grow'.* Model rereading and continue: *'To sprout' means 'to develop or grow' so this must be the answer.* You could show the children a picture of a seed sprouting to boost their understanding. Finally, model writing and checking the answer.

Word meaning questions mark scheme

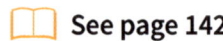

The following guidance can be used with the children if support is needed.

	Answer	Guidance
1	taller	Prompt the children to use the locator to find the correct section. You could use the steps in **Modelling question 1** to support them to answer this type of question. **Award 1 mark for the correct answer.**
2	get bigger/get taller/develop	Remind the children that they need to use the text to help them explain what 'grow' means. Ask them to scan for the first time 'grow' appears and support them to reread the relevant sentence to work out the meaning. **Award 1 mark for the correct answer.**

Answer		Guidance
3	tiny — miniature strong — tough spiky — prickly	Remind the children that they must draw clear lines to match the words on the left with their meanings on the right. You could use the steps in **Modelling question 3** to help break down this matching question. **Award 1 mark for one pair correctly matched. Award 2 marks for all pairs correctly matched.**
4	a type of round root	Prompt the children to use the locator to find the relevant section. Read and discuss the sentences that contain the word 'bulb' to facilitate understanding. The children may also mention that a bulb contains food to help the plant grow or that daffodils and tulips grow from bulbs, but this is not acceptable without the first part of the answer. **Award 1 mark for the correct answer.**

Mix it up! questions mark scheme

The following guidance can be used with the children if support is needed.

Answer		Guidance
1	fern	Point out to the children that the question asks for the name of only one kind of plant. Encourage them to find the section that mentions plants that don't need much light (**Plant habitats**) and then to write down the name of the plant. **Award 1 mark for the correct answer. Skill: Retrieval.**
2	Plant habitats [2] Parts of a plant [3] What are plants? [1] Seeds and bulbs [4]	Encourage the children to find, highlight and number the subheadings on the text before transferring them to the answer boxes. **Award 1 mark for a correct number in one box. Award 2 marks for the correct numbers in all boxes. Skill: Sequencing.**
3	It is a good name for this section because it explains that plants are living things like humans.	Explain that this is an inference question, so the answer will not be given in the text. Encourage the children to think about what subheadings are for (they tell us about what is in each part of the text so that we can find information quickly) and how the information in the text matches the subheading. **Award 1 mark for any reference to defining what plants are. Skill: Inference.**
4	Unusual plants ✓ Plants as food ✓	Encourage the children to think about likely and unlikely topics to see in a book about plants. You could show them the contents pages of some non-fiction books to demonstrate how they tackle different aspects of a topic. If necessary, point out that two of the possible answers mention plants and two do not. **Award 1 mark for both correct answers ticked. Skill: Prediction.**

Plant Facts, by Izzi Howell

What types of plant and flower have you seen in the park, at school, or in your garden, if you are lucky enough to have one? Have you ever looked after a plant? This extract from a non-fiction text is all about plants – where plants grow, the different parts of a plant, and what they need to stay alive.

What are plants?

Plants are living things. Like animals and humans, they need food and water. They grow taller and bigger and reproduce to make new plants.

Plants come in many sizes, from tall trees to tiny green algae.

Fact

Some types of algae are so small that they can only be seen through a microscope!

Plant habitats

Plants grow in many habitats around the world. Plants are often different from one habitat to another.

Spiky cactuses grow in dry deserts.

There are many types of brightly coloured flower in the rainforest.

Slimy seaweed is found in seas and oceans.

Plants that don't need much light, such as ferns, grow on the shady woodland floor.

Cactuses

Parts of a plant

Most plants have three main parts – the roots, the stem and the leaves. Each part of the plant has a different job.

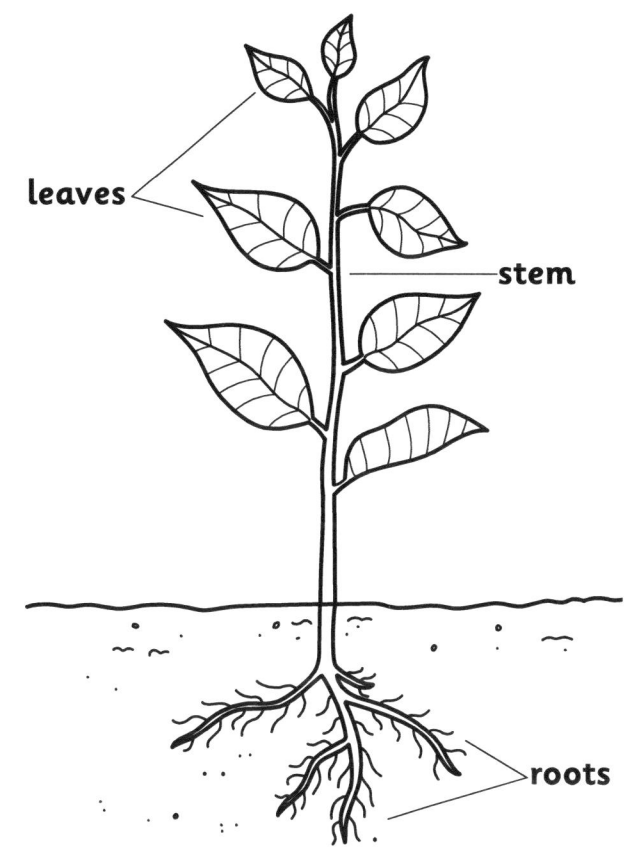

Plant roots grow underground in the soil. The stem and leaves grow above ground.

Plant roots take in water and nutrients from the soil. This water travels up the plant stem to the leaves.

The job of leaves is to make food for the plant.

Fact

Plant roots are very strong. Some can even break through stone and concrete!

Seeds and bulbs

Most plants grow from seeds. When a seed is in a dark, warm, damp place, its hard shell breaks open and it sprouts roots and a shoot.

Some plants don't grow from seeds. Plants such as daffodils and tulips grow from a type of round root, called a bulb. Bulbs are filled with food, which the plant uses to grow new leaves.

From *Plant Facts* by Izzi Howell. Reproduced by permission of Wayland Books, an imprint of Hachette Children's Books, Carmelite House, 50 Victoria Embankment, London, EC4Y 0DZ.

Word meaning

Name: _____

1 Reread the subheading **What are plants?**. Find and copy **one** word that means 'higher'.

_____

1 mark

2 What does the word *grow* mean?

_____

1 mark

3 Draw lines to match the words to their meanings.

tiny		tough
strong		prickly
spiky		miniature

2 marks

4 Reread the subheading **Seeds and bulbs**. What does *bulb* mean?

_____
_____

1 mark

Mix it up!

Name: _____

1 Which plant does not need much light?

_____

1 mark

2 Number the subheadings to show the order in which they appear in the text.

Plant habitats ☐

Parts of a plant ☐

What are plants? [1]

Seeds and bulbs ☐

2 marks

3 Look at the subheading **What are plants?**. Why is this a good name for the section?

_____
_____

1 mark

4 What other subheadings do you think a book about plants might have? Tick **two**.

How to care for your pet ☐

Unusual plants ☐

Plants as food ☐

Baking a cake ☐

1 mark

Unit 16 — Retrieval / Fiction

Jack and the Beanstalk
by Jo Gray

▽ **Printable text** • **Modelling slides**   📖 **Photocopiable text and questions** • pages 148 to 151

This retelling of the classic fairy tale has been written to allow young children to apply their phonic knowledge and read the text more independently. As the story of 'Jack and the Beanstalk' is often linked to the topic of plants in the Key Stage 1 science curriculum, you may wish to refer back to your discussions of the text in Unit 15.

① Get ready

Discuss the **Key vocabulary** identified in the **Language toolkit** and then complete the vocabulary and phonics activities as desired. Please note that the selected vocabulary is a guide. Depending on the needs of your cohort, additional vocabulary discussion may be beneficial before, during and after reading. Next, display the text (pages 148 to 149) so the children can see the title and any illustrations, and encourage the children to answer the following questions before reading.

1. **What sort of text do you think this is?**
   I think this is a fairy tale/a made-up story. Encourage the children to use the illustration to expand on their answer (e.g. *I think this is a fairy tale because there is a picture of a giant, and fairy tales are usually about magical or imaginary creatures*). Support them to understand that because the text is a story, it is a fictional text.

2. **Have you read any texts like this before?**
   Answers will vary depending on the children's experiences. Some may have heard the story before and will make links to other fairy tales that they know, such as 'Little Red Riding Hood' (see Unit 7) and 'The Three Little Pigs' (see Units 9 and 10). Some may make links to stories about giants; others may make links to stories about plants growing (see the **Reading list** for some examples).

3. **Why do you think the title mentions a beanstalk?**
   Answers will vary depending on the children's familiarity with the story. Some children may be able to recall part of the story; others may talk about growing plants and caring for them. Allow them to explore different reasons and expand on their ideas.

Language toolkit

Key vocabulary

amazed	angry	cupboard
gigantic	impressed	magic
money	suddenly	supper

Vocabulary discussion questions

- What do you normally have for your **supper**?
- Have your friends ever been **impressed** with something you've done?
- Would you rather have **money** or **magic** beans? Why?

Vocabulary activities

Discuss which sentence makes the most sense.

1. Mum was **angry** because I broke her plate. OR Mum was **angry** because I was good.
2. The elephant was **gigantic** compared to the mouse. OR The **suddenly** was **gigantic**.

Phonics

Year 1 phonics	climb, grown, market, poor, threw
Split digraphs	take, inside, outside, time, woke
Common exception words	he, his, no, once, one, she, some, the, there, was, were

Phonics activity

Ask the children to correct the sentence below.

The jiant fel asleep so jack ran hoem

The children should add a full stop to the end. Many will also correct the spelling of 'giant', 'fell' and 'home'. Some may spot that 'jack' needs a capital letter because it is a name.

2 First steps

Read the text together and then encourage the children to discuss the following questions.

1. **Who is in the story?**
   The characters in the story are Jack, Jack's mother, the old man and the giant. Some children may also mention the cow, the hen and the harp.

2. **What did Jack's mother do when she saw the beans?**
   She threw them out of the window (and sent Jack to bed without any supper). You could challenge the children to tell you how they think Jack's mother was feeling when she acted in this way (e.g. upset, angry).

3. **What was unusual about the beans?**
   They were magic. A giant beanstalk grew from them overnight. Usually it takes longer for a beanstalk to grow and it doesn't reach the clouds.

3 Explore

- Ask the children to tell you what they know about plants. You could refer back to your discussions of the text in Unit 15. Allow the children time to compare what they know about plants in real life to what happens with the beanstalk in this story.

- Give each child a pot, some soil and a bean and guide them through planting and watering their own beanstalk. Encourage the children to care for these plants. Have a class competition to see who can grow the tallest beanstalk. (This activity could link to the **Where next?** speaking and listening task in Unit 15.)

- Discuss examples of magic objects in this text (e.g. beans, harp, hen, giant) and in other traditional tales (e.g. magic mirror in 'Snow White and the Seven Dwarfs'; a magical fairy godmother in 'Cinderella'. You could link the discussion back to Units 5, 6, 7, 9 and 10, which all feature talking animals.

4 Skills focus   See pages 146 to 147

Use the information from the **Skills guide** and the relevant **Skills graphic** to introduce the skill of retrieval.

1. Model the skill using the **Unit 16 Modelling slides** and the **Modelling retrieval** guidance on page 146.

2. The children could then attempt the optional **Retrieval** questions on page 150. This may be in small groups with adult support as needed.

3. Finally, the optional **Mix it up!** questions on page 151 offer practice in a range of comprehension skills. For guidance on introducing this new activity, see page 10.

Answers and marking guidance for all questions are included on pages 146 to 147.

5 Where next?

- **Speaking and listening task:** Explore the emotions of Jack and the giant through a 'hot seat' activity. In this activity, a child plays a character and is interviewed by the rest of the class or group. The children could take turns to sit in the 'hot seat' and answer questions in character. Questions to Jack might be: *Why did you hide in the cupboard? What made you take the hen and the harp? Do you think it was the right thing to do?* Questions to the giant might be: *How did you feel when you smelt a boy in your kitchen? What would you have done if you had seen him? Why did you chase Jack? Where have you been since Jack's mother cut down the beanstalk?*

- **Writing task:** Using the information from the activity above, the children could write some sentences to retell the story from Jack's or the giant's point of view.

Reading list

Class reads
- *The Enormous Turnip* by Katie Daynes
- *The Gigantic Turnip* by Aleksei Tolstoy
- *Jack and the Jelly Bean Stalk* by Rachael Mortimer
- *Jim and the Beanstalk* by Raymond Briggs
- *Oliver's Vegetables* by Vivian French
- *The Smartest Giant in Town* by Julia Donaldson
- *Trust Me, Jack's Beanstalk Stinks! The Story of Jack and the Beanstalk as Told by the Giant* by Eric Braun

Independent reads
- *Jack and the Beanstalk* by Iona Treahy
- *Jack and the Beanstalk* by Barbara Vagnozzi
- *Hungry Plants* by Mary Batten

Non-fiction
- *The Amazing Plant Life Cycle Story* by Kay Barnham
- *Perfectly Peculiar Plants* by Chris Thorogood
- *Plant Facts* by Izzi Howell (Linked text: Unit 15)
- *Secrets of the Vegetable Garden* by Carron Brown
- *Wild Things: Over 100 Magical Outdoor Adventures* by Jo Schofield and Fiona Danks

Poetry
- *There Was an Old Giant Who Swallowed a Clock* by Becky Davies

Websites
- The BBC School Radio website tells the story of 'Jack and the Beanstalk' through 14 short video clips.

Schofield & Sims Complete Comprehension 1

Unit 16

Modelling retrieval

▽ See Unit 16 Modelling slides

Use the **Skills guide** (see pages 16 to 17) and the downloadable **Skills graphic** to support your modelling.

1 Who did Jack sell the cow to?

the old man

Think aloud: *Jack sells the cow early on in the story, so I will look at the first part again.* Model scanning for the key words 'cow' and 'sell' to locate the relevant part ('Jack had to take their cow to market and sell her.'). Continue: *I need to read on and see who Jack sells the cow to.* Model reading further. Continue: *I think the answer to the question is here – 'Jack sold the cow to the old man'*. Model writing and checking the answer.

2 Which events happened in the story? Tick two.

Jack's mother sold the cow.	☐
Jack took the giant's hen.	✓
The giant ate Jack.	☐
A beanstalk grew in the night.	✓

Think aloud: *As I have already read the story, I think I know what does and does not happen. However, it's very important to check against the text.* Discuss each event in turn: *The first one says that Jack's mother sold the cow – I don't think that is correct – it was Jack.* Repeat for the other statements. Model checking that you have chosen the right statements by scanning the text for key words and pointing to the evidence. Finally, model ticking two answers.

3 How did Jack feel when he heard the giant enter the kitchen?

scared

Encourage the children to find the part of the text where the giant enters the kitchen. Think aloud: *The question asks how Jack felt, so I am looking for a feeling. Here it says, 'Jack felt scared'. Let me check the question to see if this answers it.* Model rereading the question: *Yes, Jack was scared when he heard the giant and we know he is in the kitchen because it says, 'He ran and hid inside a gigantic cupboard in the kitchen'.* Model writing and checking the answer.

4 What did the giant say to the hen? Tick one.

"Fee, fi, fo, fum!"	☐
"Lay!"	✓
"Sing!"	☐
"I smell the blood of a little boy!"	☐

Think aloud: *I know I can only tick one answer. I need to look for the part of the text where the giant talks to the hen.* Model skim-reading the text and highlighting the relevant section. Continue: *It says, '"Lay!" said the giant to the hen', so the answer must be "Lay!".* You could discuss why the answer is not any of the other statements, despite these being things that the giant said in the course of the story. Model ticking the answer and checking it against the question.

Retrieval questions mark scheme

📖 See page 150

The following guidance can be used with the children if support is needed.

	Answer	Guidance
1	in a castle	Prompt the children to look for key words in the question and then find the relevant part of the text. Support them to skim-read the paragraphs before and after the first mention of the giant. **Award 1 mark for the correct answer.**

Jack and the Beanstalk, by Jo Gray

	Answer	Guidance
2	The giant had a golden harp. ✓ The giant climbed down the beanstalk. ✓	Remind the children of **Modelling question 2**. The children should take each statement in turn and scan the text for it, highlighting the two events that occur. **Award 1 mark for one correct answer ticked. Award 2 marks for both correct answers ticked.**
3	The harp sang a song. ✓	Encourage the children to find the part of the text where the giant is asleep. Prompt them to then scan for the part where the giant wakes up. They should then look at the previous sentence and think about what woke the giant up. Remind them to tick one answer only. **Award 1 mark for the correct answer ticked.**
4	Nobody saw him again. ✓	Ask the children to point to the end of the text (the final paragraph). Ask them to scan for the sentence that mentions the giant. Remind them to tick one answer only. **Award 1 mark for the correct answer ticked.**

Mix it up! questions mark scheme

See page 151

The following guidance can be used with the children if support is needed.

	Answer	Guidance
1	gigantic *and* enormous	If necessary, encourage the children to skim-read the text looking for adjectives that describe height. Can they think of any 'huge' things mentioned in the story? They could discuss their choices with a partner before writing them down. **Award 1 mark for each correct answer.** Skill: Word meaning.
2	Jack swapped the cow for magic beans. [1] The giant fell asleep. [4] Jack hid from the giant. [3] Jack escaped from the giant. [5] Jack climbed the beanstalk. [2]	If necessary, encourage the children to find, highlight and number all the events in the text before transferring them to the answer boxes. **Award 1 mark for the correct numbers in at least two boxes. Award 2 marks for the correct numbers in all boxes.** Skill: Sequencing.
3	Jack had taken something that didn't belong to him. ✓	If necessary, ask the children to find the event mentioned in the question in the text. Ask them if they would feel cross if someone took one of their favourite toys without asking. Why would they feel this way? Encourage them to relate their feelings to the possible answers. Remind them to tick one answer only. **Award 1 mark for the correct answer.** Skill: Inference.
4	Jack's mother would feel happy because having golden eggs would mean that she would not be poor any more.	If necessary, encourage the children to think about what they know about Jack's mother (she was poor/sad because she had no money) and what the hen might help with (money – because it could lay golden eggs). **Award 1 mark for a plausible prediction.** Skill: Prediction.

Jack and the Beanstalk, by Jo Gray

Have you ever planted a bean? How long did it take to grow? What would you do if you planted a bean and when you woke up the next day there was a beanstalk that was taller than the clouds? This is exactly what happened to Jack.

Once upon a time there was a boy called Jack. He lived with his mother. They were very poor. All they had was a cow.

One morning, Jack's mother was sad. She told Jack they had no money. Jack had to take their cow to market and sell her.

On the way, Jack met an old man who wanted to buy their cow. He had no money but he gave Jack some magic beans in exchange for the cow. Jack sold the cow to the old man.

When Jack's mother saw the beans she was very angry. She threw the beans out of the window and sent Jack to bed without any supper.

The next morning, Jack looked out of the window. A gigantic beanstalk had grown. It was higher than the clouds. Jack went outside and started to climb the beanstalk. He climbed up to the sky. At the top of the beanstalk, Jack saw a beautiful castle and went inside.

Jack was impressed with how big everything was in the castle! Suddenly, he heard a voice. "Fee, fi, fo, fum! I smell the blood of a little boy!" Jack felt scared. He ran and hid inside a gigantic cupboard in the kitchen.

An enormous giant came into the room. He couldn't see Jack so he sat down at the table. On the table there was a large hen. "Lay!" said the giant to the hen.

At once, the hen laid an egg. It was made of gold! There was also a golden harp on the table. "Sing!" said the giant, and the harp began to sing. Jack was amazed. He wished he could have something like that to stop his mother being poor and sad.

The harp sang until the giant fell asleep. Jack jumped out of the cupboard and took the hen and the harp.

Suddenly, the harp sang a song!

The giant woke up and shouted, "Fee, fi, fo, fum! I smell the blood of a little boy!"

Jack ran as fast as he could and started to climb down the beanstalk. The giant saw that Jack had taken his hen and his harp and he was very cross. He began to climb down after Jack. Jack reached the bottom and shouted, "Mother! Help!"

Jack's mother took an axe and chopped down the beanstalk. Nobody ever saw the giant again. With the golden eggs and the magic harp, Jack and his mother were no longer poor or sad, and they lived happily ever after.

Retrieval

Name: _____

1 Where did the giant live?

_____

1 mark

2 Which events happened in the story? Tick **two**.

The giant had a golden harp. ☐

The giant laid an egg. ☐

The giant climbed down the beanstalk. ☐

The giant hid in a cupboard. ☐

2 marks

3 What woke the giant up? Tick **one**.

He smelt a magic bean. ☐

The hen laid an egg. ☐

The harp sang a song. ☐

He was hungry. ☐

1 mark

4 What happened to the giant at the end of the story? Tick **one**.

He got his hen and his harp back. ☐

Nobody saw him again. ☐

He went back to his castle. ☐

He lived with Jack. ☐

1 mark

Mix it up!

Name: _____

1 Find and copy **two** words that mean the same as 'huge'.

_____ and _____   2 marks

2 Number the events to show the order in which they happened in the story. One has been done for you.

Jack swapped the cow for magic beans.   [1]

The giant fell asleep.   [ ]

Jack hid from the giant.   [ ]

Jack escaped from the giant.   [ ]

Jack climbed the beanstalk.   [ ]

2 marks

3 *The giant saw that Jack had taken his hen and his harp and he was very cross.* Why do you think the giant was cross? Tick **one**.

The harp had woken the giant up.   [ ]

Jack had taken something that didn't belong to him.   [ ]

He wanted to get to the beanstalk first.   [ ]

He wanted to give his hen a hug.   [ ]

1 mark

4 How do you think Jack's mother would feel if she saw that the hen could lay golden eggs? Why?

_____

_____   1 mark

Photocopiable resource from *Complete Comprehension 1* © Schofield & Sims Ltd, 2020.

Unit 16 — Jack and the Beanstalk, by Jo Gray

Unit 17

My Two Grannies
by Floella Benjamin

Printable text • **Modelling slides**   **Photocopiable text and questions** • **pages 156 to 159**

Inference • Fiction

My Two Grannies is a book that explores differences between places and people at a level that children in Year 1 can understand. In this story, Alvina has two grannies: Granny Vero from the Caribbean island of Trinidad, and Granny Rose from the north of England. This text is an excellent opportunity to make links to the geography curriculum for this age group by comparing beaches in different countries. You could also use this text to discuss culture, heritage and how everyone is different.

1 Get ready

Discuss the **Key vocabulary** identified in the **Language toolkit** and then complete the vocabulary and phonics activities as desired. Please note that the selected vocabulary is a guide. Depending on the needs of your cohort, additional vocabulary discussion may be beneficial before, during and after reading. Next, display the text (pages 156 to 157) so the children can see the title and any illustrations, and encourage the children to discuss the following questions before reading.

1. **What sort of text do you think this is? What do you think it might be about?**
   Looking at the picture, I think it is a story about family. It might be about a girl and her grandparents. Support the children to understand that because the text is a story, it is an example of a fictional text.

2. **Have you read any texts like this before?**
   Answers will vary depending on the children's experiences. Some will make links to stories that include family members; others may refer to texts that explore other cultures, such as *Handa's Surprise* by Eileen Browne, *Amazing Grace* by Mary Hoffman or *Gregory Cool* by Caroline Binch.

3. **Looking at the Key vocabulary, what do you think the story will be about?**
   Answers will vary depending on the children's understanding of the vocabulary. Some may suggest that the story will talk about lots of different places; others may mention holidays or beaches. They may also refer to the text's title and illustration and talk about the girl and her grannies. You may wish to look at these places on a map. This is also covered in **Explore**.

Language toolkit

Key vocabulary

Barnsley	beach	Blackpool
Caribbean	city	island
Trinidad	tropical	Yorkshire

Vocabulary discussion questions

- Which is bigger: a town or a **city**?
- What is the opposite of **tropical**?
- Have you ever been to a **beach**?

Vocabulary activities

Discuss which sentence makes the most sense.

1. An **island** is surrounded by water. OR
   An **island** has no **beaches**.
2. A **beach** is where cows and sheep live. OR
   A **beach** is by the sea.

Phonics

Year 1 phonics	city, forward, heart, promise, would
Split digraphs	Rose, age, face, same, take, ride, smile
Common exception words	and, go, her, love, of, one, said, she, the, they, to, was, were, you

Phonics activity

Ask the children to correct the sentence below.

the see in blackpool wos much to cowld
The children should add a capital letter to the start and a full stop to the end. Most will correct the spelling of 'sea' and 'was' and will add the capital letter to 'Blackpool'. Some may also correct 'cold' and 'too'.

2 First steps

Read the text together and then encourage the children to discuss the following questions.

1 Where was Granny Vero born?
   Granny Vero was born on a Caribbean island called Trinidad.

2 Where was Granny Rose born?
   Granny Rose was born in Barnsley, which is in Yorkshire.

3 Where do both grannies live now?
   Both grannies live in the same city as Alvina now.

3 Explore

- Look at a map of the world and find Trinidad. Then look at where Barnsley and Blackpool are. Using the internet, look at how far it is from Trinidad to Barnsley (4397 miles). Point out that it would take nearly a day to fly there in a plane. Put the distance of one mile into context for the children by describing a short journey in their local area.

- Show the children images or a video clip of both Blackpool and Trinidad. Ask them to discuss what they think is the same and what they think is different about the two places. Then draw a comparison chart on the board with 'Similarities' and 'Differences' as the column headings. Add an example under each heading: (e.g. 'sea' under 'Similarities' and 'weather' under 'Differences'). Fill in the chart with the children's help.

- If you want to explore the differences further, you could compare traditional Caribbean meals with traditional British meals. The children could look at some images or menus and discuss the differences between the two cuisines.

4 Skills focus   See pages 154 to 155

Use the information from the **Skills guide** and the relevant **Skills graphic** to introduce the skill of inference.

1 Model the skill using the **Unit 17 Modelling slides** and the **Modelling inference** guidance on page 154.

2 The children could then attempt the optional **Inference** questions on page 158. This may be in small groups with adult support as needed.

3 Finally, the optional **Mix it up!** questions on page 159 offer practice in a range of comprehension skills.

Answers and marking guidance for all questions are included on pages 154 to 155.

5 Where next?

Speaking and listening task: Explore vocabulary you might use at the beach. The children could think about a location from the story or draw on their own experiences. Generate a list (e.g. sandcastle, bucket, spade, donkey ride, ice cream, sea, waves, towel, shell, crab, fish, rocks). In pairs, the children could then use the vocabulary to role-play a conversation they might have on the beach (e.g. buying an ice cream; building a sandcastle; paddling in the sea; asking for a donkey ride; exploring a rock pool).

Writing task: Show the children images and play them recordings of a beach environment. What can they see and hear? Ask them to use these ideas and the words from the activity above to write a postcard to a relative, pretending they are on holiday.

Reading list

Class reads
- *Amazing Grace* by Mary Hoffman
- *Gregory Cool* by Caroline Binch
- *Handa's Surprise* by Eileen Browne
- *The Lighthouse Keeper's Lunch* by Ronda Armitage
- *My Caribbean Grandma* by Sandra Campbell-Notice
- *The Secret of Spiggy Holes* by Enid Blyton
- *Tales from the Caribbean* by Trish Cooke

Independent reads
- *Flotsam* by David Wiesner (wordless picture book)
- *Grandad Mandela* by Zazi, Ziwelene and Zindzi Mandela (Linked text: Unit 18)
- *I Love Saturdays y Domingos* by Alma Flor Ada
- *My Two Grandads* by Floella Benjamin
- *Who's In My Family? All About Our Families* by Robie H. Harris

Non-fiction
- *Next Stop: The Caribbean* by Ginger McDonnell
- *100 Facts: Seashore* by Steve Parker
- *Seaside Holidays (Ways Into History)* by Sally Hewitt
- *The Seaside: Then and Now* by Gill Stacey and Liz Paren

Poetry
- *A Caribbean Dozen* by John Agard and Grace Nichols (eds)
- *Seaside Poems* by Jill Bennett
- *Under the Moon and Over the Sea: A Collection of Poetry from the Caribbean* by John Agard and Grace Nichols (eds)

Websites
- The Science for Kids website contains a list of fun facts about beaches.

Modelling inference

△ See Unit 17 Modelling slides

Use the **Skills guide** (see pages 20 to 21) and the downloadable **Skills graphic** to support your modelling.

1 **Why did Granny Vero have a big smile on her face when she talked about splashing in the sea?**

   Granny Vero was happy because she was thinking about how she used to enjoy splashing in the warm sea.

   Model identifying the key words (e.g. Granny Vero, smile, sea) and scanning for them to find and highlight the relevant part of the text. Think aloud: *If I was smiling, it would be because I was happy. I think Granny Vero was smiling because she was thinking about something that made her happy when she was younger. Now I need to write this in a sentence.* Model writing the answer with the children's input and checking it against the question.

2 **Why did Alvina beg Granny Vero to tell her the story about Trinidad again? Tick one.**

   Alvina didn't want to hear the story. ☐
   Alvina loved hearing the story again and again. ☑
   Alvina was cold. ☐
   Alvina had forgotten the story. ☐

   Identify the key words in the question (e.g. 'beg', 'tell', 'again', 'tick one'). Model scanning for them to find the relevant part of the text. Think aloud: *Why might you beg to hear a story again?* (because you enjoy hearing it). Continue: *Which of the possible answers is most similar to this?* Model ticking one answer only and checking it against the question.

3 **How did Granny Rose feel about going to Blackpool Beach when she was younger? How do you know?**

   I think she liked it because she suggests that they should all go to the beach for the day.

   Explain to the children that 'How do you know?' is an extra part of this question, and that you need to give an answer for each part. Find and highlight the correct part of the text. Think aloud: *I think Granny Rose liked Blackpool. Are there any examples in the text that show this?* Encourage the children to discuss their ideas. Continue: *Granny Rose played on the beach 'all day long' so she must have enjoyed herself. Is there anything else?* Discuss how she invites everyone to the beach. Continue: *I think this shows she liked it there, as she wants to share it with others.* Model writing an answer and checking it.

4 **How do you know that Alvina thought that the sea in Blackpool was warm, like it is in Trinidad?**

   I know because she asked Granny Rose if she spent all day in the sea in Blackpool.

   Identify the key words in the question ('How do you know'/'Alvina'/'sea'/'Blackpool'/'warm'). Model scanning for the relevant part of the text and think aloud: *If I was unsure about something, I might ask a question. Here, Alvina asks Granny Rose if she spent all day in the sea.* Encourage the children to discuss why Alvina might ask this (because Granny Vero spent all day in the sea, and Alvina didn't know that Blackpool was not hot like Trinidad). Model writing the answer with the children's input and checking it against the question.

Inference questions mark scheme

📖 See page 158

The following guidance can be used with the children if support is needed.

	Answer	Guidance
1	She wanted to stay in the warm water because it was so much fun splashing around.	If necessary, encourage the children to identify the key words in the question and scan for them. Encourage them to think about why they would want to continue doing something. **Award 1 mark for any reference to Granny Vero enjoying the water. Do not accept answers that only mention the water being warm.**

Answer			Guidance
2	because it was too cold to spend all day in the sea	✓	Encourage the children to highlight the relevant part of the text. Prompt them to use the text to help them decide which of the possible answers explains why Granny Rose laughed. If necessary, point out that no jokes are told in the text. **Award 1 mark for the correct answer ticked.**
3	Granny Vero liked the Caribbean. I know this because she smiled when she talked about it and she said she would go back to visit with Alvina.		If necessary, support the children to highlight the relevant part of the text. Encourage them to think about how Granny Vero acted when she talked about the Caribbean (she smiled). **Award 1 mark for any reference to Granny Vero liking/loving the Caribbean. Award another mark for any reference to Vero smiling when talking about Trinidad or enjoying the sea there.**
4	Alvina always looked forward to visiting her grannies. *OR* Alvina loved hearing their stories.		If necessary, point out that the question asks for one example, even if there are more to give. Encourage the children to look for clues in the text that show that Alvina enjoyed being with her grannies. Remind them to check their answer against the question. The children are not required to give a direct quote – accept any relevant example written in their own words. **Award 1 mark for one correct answer.**

Mix it up! questions mark scheme   See page 159

Answer			Guidance
1	*tropical* and *warm*		If necessary, encourage the children to think of words that mean 'hot' and to look for them in the text. You could remind them of the **Key vocabulary** word 'tropical'. **Award 1 mark for each correct answer. Skill: Word meaning.**
2	rode a donkey.	✓	If necessary, explain that the answer to this retrieval question will be found in the text. Encourage the children to find and highlight the answer in the text before ticking it. **Award 1 mark for the correct answer ticked. Skill: Retrieval.**
3	Granny Rose told Alvina about Blackpool Beach.	4	If necessary, encourage the children to find, highlight and number the events in the text before filling in the answer boxes. **Award 1 mark for the correct numbers in at least two boxes. Award 2 marks for the correct numbers in all boxes. Skill: Sequencing.**
	Granny Vero promised to take Alvina to Trinidad.	3	
	Granny Vero told Alvina about playing in the sea all day.	2	
	Alvina begged Granny Vero to tell her about Trinidad.	1	
	Granny Rose said that they should all go to Blackpool.	5	
4	I don't think she would like it because she is used to the sea being warm. *OR* I think she would like seeing the beach in Blackpool and comparing it with the beach in Trinidad.		If necessary, explain that the children need to make a prediction. Encourage them to first decide if Granny Vero would like Blackpool or not. Then encourage them to think about why. Remind them to check their answer against the question. **Award 1 mark for a plausible prediction. Skill: Prediction.**

My Two Grannies, by Floella Benjamin

Where were your parents born? What about your grandparents? Some children have family members that all come from the same country, or even the same town, as them. Others have family members who were born in different countries. The girl in this extract has both! Where our families come from is something that makes us all different – yet we all share similarities, too.

Alvina had two grannies who she loved with all her heart. They were called Granny Vero and Granny Rose.

Granny Vero was born on the Caribbean island of Trinidad and Granny Rose was born in the Yorkshire town of Barnsley. Now they both lived in the same city as Alvina and her parents.

Alvina always looked forward to visiting her grannies because she loved hearing the stories they told about when they were little girls.

"Tell me about Trinidad again," Alvina begged.

"Don't you ever get tired of hearing the same stories, Alvina?" said Granny Vero.

"Never!" said Alvina.

"When I was your age we would go to the beach, and splash around in the tropical sea," said Granny Vero, with a big smile on her face.

"We never wanted to come out of that warm water."

"I would love to do that, Granny V," said Alvina.

"Well, one day I will take you to Trinidad, darlin'," said Granny Vero. "I promise."

When Alvina saw Granny Rose, she asked, "Did you swim in the sea all day when you were little?"

"No, luvvie," laughed Granny Rose. "The sea in Blackpool was much too cold. But we did play on the beach all day long and ride on the donkeys. We must all go to Blackpool one day so you can do that too."

"Oh, yes please!" said Alvina.

From *My Two Grannies* by Floella Benjamin, published by Frances Lincoln Ltd, copyright © 2007. Reproduced by permission of Frances Lincoln Ltd, an imprint of The Quarto Group.

Inference

Name: _____

1 Why did Granny Vero want to stay in the warm sea water?

_____

1 mark

2 Why do you think Granny Rose laughed when Alvina asked her if she spent all day in the sea? Tick **one**.

because she told a joke ☐

because she couldn't swim ☐

because it was too cold to spend all day in the sea ☐

because she was hot ☐

1 mark

3 How did Granny Vero feel about Trinidad? How do you know?

_____

_____

2 marks

4 Give **one** example from the story that shows that Alvina liked spending time with her grannies.

_____

1 mark

Mix it up!

Name: _____

1 Find and copy **two** words that tell you that the sea in Trinidad was hot.

_____ and _____   2 marks

2 What did Granny Rose do on the beach? Tick **one**.

Granny Rose …

built sandcastles. ☐

paddled in the sea. ☐

rode a horse. ☐

rode a donkey. ☐

1 mark

3 Number the events to show the order in which they happened in the story. One has been done for you.

Granny Rose told Alvina about Blackpool Beach. ☐

Granny Vero promised to take Alvina to Trinidad. ☐

Granny Vero told Alvina about playing in the sea all day. ☐

Alvina begged Granny Vero to tell her about Trinidad. [1]

Granny Rose said that they should all go to Blackpool. ☐

2 marks

4 Do you think Granny Vero would like Blackpool? Explain your answer.

_____

_____

1 mark

Unit 17

My Two Grannies, by Floella Benjamin

Photocopiable resource from *Complete Comprehension 1* © Schofield & Sims Ltd, 2020.

Grandad Mandela
by Zazi, Ziwelene and Zindzi Mandela

▽ Printable text • Modelling slides   📖 Photocopiable text and questions • pages 164 to 167

Like *My Two Grannies* in Unit 17, this text also explores the relationship between grandparents and their grandchildren. Taken from a powerful, emotive non-fiction narrative, this extract sees Nelson Mandela's two great-grandchildren asking their grandmother questions about her father and learning about what he was fighting for. This text provides a fantastic opportunity to explore a significant event in history through a child's perspective.

❶ Get ready

Discuss the **Key vocabulary** identified in the **Language toolkit** and then complete the vocabulary and phonics activities as desired. Please note that the selected vocabulary is a guide. Depending on the needs of your cohort, additional vocabulary discussion may be beneficial before, during and after reading. Next, display the text (pages 164 to 165) so the children can see the title and any illustrations, and encourage the children to answer the following questions before reading.

1. **What sort of text do you think this is?**
   It is worth spending some time on this question. Many children are likely to suggest that it is fiction or a made-up story, but the text is in fact a retelling of real-life events.

2. **Have you read any texts like this before?**
   The children may draw links with the previous text, *My Two Grannies*, and discuss the relationship between grandparents and their grandchildren. A few children may understand the significance of the name Grandad Mandela.

3. **Looking at the Key vocabulary words, what do you think the text will be about?**
   Answers will vary. Support the children to come up with some suggestions (e.g. *This text will be about somebody breaking the law or going to jail for fighting; This text is about somebody who is different*).

Language toolkit

Key vocabulary

against	apartheid*	different
equal	fighting	jail
law	remembered	separated

*Apartheid is discussed in **Explore**.

Vocabulary discussion questions

- Why would somebody go to **jail**?
- How might you feel if you were **separated** from your best friend?
- What does it mean to be **equal** to somebody else?

Vocabulary activities

Discuss which sentence makes the most sense.

1. Max still **remembered** his first ever teddy. OR I couldn't go swimming because I **remembered** my kit.
2. Be good and don't break the **law**. OR Be good and break the **law**.

Phonics

Year 1 phonics	about, course, found, house, know, replied, taste
Split digraphs	same, like, white
Common exception words	and, asked, be, he, love, my, of, one, said, they, was, we, were, you

Phonics activity

Ask the children to correct the sentence below.

Why did Grandad gow too jayl asked Zazi.
The children should correct the spelling of 'go', 'to' and 'jail'. Some may suggest adding the speech marks and a question mark after 'jail'.

2 First steps

Read the text together and then encourage the children to discuss the following questions.

1. Where were Zazi and Ziwelene playing?
   They were playing at their grandma's house.
2. Who did the children find a photograph of?
   They found a photograph of their Grandad Mandela.
3. What similarities do you notice between this text and the previous text, *My Two Grannies*?
   Both stories talk about the children and their grandparents. You could encourage the children to expand on their answers (e.g. 'Alvina in *My Two Grannies* and the children in this story both like hearing stories about their grandparents' lives').

3 Explore

- Ask the children if they know who Grandad Mandela was. Show them a photograph of Nelson Mandela and explain that he came from South Africa (point this out on a map). Explain that Mandela spent time in prison for standing up for what he believed in: that black and white people should be treated equally. This was during a time in the past when a law called apartheid separated black people in South Africa from white people and treated them very badly. Nelson Mandela thought that this was wrong and he fought to make life better for black people. When he was released from jail, Mandela became the first black president of South Africa. Many people believe that he was a great leader because he helped to bring the country together.

- Depending on your cohort, you could explore apartheid in more detail using the following exercise: put 30 counters (or as many as there are pupils in your class) in a bag. Twenty-five are one colour and five are another colour. The children pick a counter at random. The five children who draw the second colour are allowed to play/have a snack, whereas the other 25 children must sit and watch/continue with their classwork. After a short time (five minutes maximum), bring the class back together and ask the larger group of children how they felt, and relate this to how unfair it must have felt to live during apartheid. Before moving on, ensure that you allow the other group of children to have the same playtime/snack.

- Discuss Grandma Zindzi's words: "You know like we say, 'I Love You Lots Like Jelly Tots'? We are different colours but we all taste the same?" Ask the children what they think Grandma means. Discuss that Jelly Tots are jelly sweets that come in lots of different colours. Elicit the idea that although people can look different (e.g. different skin/hair colours) we are all alike because we are all people, and everyone should be treated equally because we are equally important – we need lots of different people in our world or it would be a boring place!

4 Skills focus   See pages 162 to 163

Use the information from the **Skills guide** and the relevant **Skills graphic** to introduce the skill of word meaning.

1. Model the skill using the **Unit 18 Modelling slides** and the **Modelling word meaning** guidance on page 162.
2. The children could then attempt the optional **Word meaning** questions on page 166. This may be in small groups with adult support as needed.
3. Finally, the optional **Mix it up!** questions on page 167 offer practice in a range of comprehension skills.

Answers and marking guidance for all questions are included on pages 162 to 163.

5 Where next?

- **Speaking and listening task:** Ask the children to imagine that a decision has been made in school that is unfair to a group of people (e.g. Year 1 are not allowed playtime but all other year groups are). What would they say if this was true? How would they stand up for what they believe in? Encourage the children to come up with statements using the vocabulary for this unit (e.g. *We are no different from the other children. We should be treated equally*).

- **Writing task:** Following on from the activity above, encourage the children to make a poster about respect and treating all people equally.

Reading list

Class reads
▶ *Little Guides to Great Lives: Nelson Mandela* by Isabel Thomas

Independent reads
▶ *Long Walk to Freedom: Illustrated Children's Edition* abridged by Chris Van Wyk
▶ *My Two Grannies* by Floella Benjamin (Linked text: Unit 17)

Non-fiction
▶ *Introducing Africa* by Chris Oxlade
▶ *Nelson Mandela* by Barbara Kramer
▶ *Who Was Nelson Mandela?* by Meg Belviso

Poetry
▶ *Poems About Families* by Brian Moses

Modelling word meaning

See Unit 18 Modelling slides

Use the **Skills guide** (see pages 14 to 15) and the downloadable **Skills graphic** to support your modelling.

1 **Find and copy one word from the story that means 'unalike'.**
   different

   Model rereading the question and identifying the key words. Think aloud: *I need to copy a word that means 'unalike'. Do we know any words that mean something similar to 'unalike'?* Model scanning the text and then read: *'We are different colours …'*. Continue to think aloud: *To be different means to be not the same or unalike. I think the answer is 'different'*. Model writing the answer and checking it against the question.

2 **Which word from the story means 'rule'? Tick one.**

   different ☐
   equal ☐
   law ✓
   jail ☐

   Model rereading the question and point out that you can only tick one answer. Scan for and highlight the possible answers in the text. Then model replacing each of the highlighted words with 'rule' and reading the new sentence (e.g. 'We are *rule* colours but we all taste the same?'). Discuss which makes the most sense. If necessary, discuss the meaning of the word 'law', which the children encountered in the **Get ready** session. Model ticking and checking the answer.

3 **"'I Love You Lots Like Jelly Tots'." What does Grandma Zindzi mean when she says this?**
   Grandma loves her grandchildren very much.

   Model finding the sentence in the text and highlighting it. Think aloud: *We know that Jelly Tots are a type of sweet, so Grandma is saying 'I love you lots like I love yummy sweets'. If someone said this to me, I would know that they loved me very much.* Model writing an answer with the children's input and checking it against the question.

4 **The author uses the word *apartheid*. What does it mean?**
   Apartheid was a law that treated white people better than black people.

   Model scanning for the word 'apartheid' in the text and highlighting it. Discuss the meaning of the word with the children, and read the whole sentence from the text: *Apartheid was a law in South Africa that separated black people and white people, and said that white people were better.* You could refer back to your activity in the **Explore** session at this point. Model writing an answer and checking it against the question.

Word meaning questions mark scheme

See page 166

The following guidance can be used with the children if support is needed.

Answer		Guidance
1	equal	Prompt the children to identify the key words in the question. Remind them that they need to find a word that means 'the same'. If necessary, support them to find the sentence 'Grandad was fighting for us all to be equal'. Discuss the fact that to be equal is similar to being the same. **Award 1 mark for the correct answer.**

Answer		Guidance
2	remembered ✓	Encourage the children to read the question and point out that this time the question asks for a word that means the opposite. Discuss the meaning of 'forgotten' and what its opposite might be. Encourage the children to tell you which possible answer makes the most sense. Remind them to tick one answer only. **Award 1 mark for the correct answer ticked.**
3	again	Encourage the children to scan for the relevant sentence. Remind them that the question asks for one word only. Encourage them to think about what each word in the sentence means. Discuss how 'again' means 'another time' or 'once more'. **Award 1 mark for the correct answer.**
4	split up/detached/apart/not together	Support the children to scan for the word 'separated' in the text and discuss its meaning. Remind them of your discussion of the Key vocabulary. **Award 1 mark for the correct answer.**

Mix it up! questions mark scheme   📖 See page 167

The following guidance can be used with the children if support is needed.

Answer		Guidance
1	because he was fighting against apartheid/the law/he was fighting for everyone to be equal	Encourage the children to scan for and highlight the part of the text that mentions Mandela going to jail. You could explain that this is a retrieval question and remind them that the answer will be in the text. **Award 1 mark for any reference to Mandela fighting against apartheid.** Skill: Retrieval.
2	The children were playing. ✓	Explain to the children that this is a sequencing question and that they should scan the text for the events given in the possible answers and number them. Encourage them to decide which event came first. Remind them to tick one answer only. **Award 1 mark for the correct answer ticked.** Skill: Sequencing.
3	It was someone they remembered very well. OR "We found a picture of Grandad Mandela."	Point out to the children that this is an unusual inference question because the answer will be found in the text. However, they will still need to use clues from the text to work out which is the right sentence. Encourage them to find the event in the text by scanning for 'photograph' and think about which sentences give us a clue that the children knew who was in the photograph. **Award 1 mark for a correct answer.** Skill: Inference.
4	ask more questions about Grandad Mandela's life ✓	Explain that this is a prediction question so the answer will not be in the text. The children need to use clues from the text to help them choose the correct answer. Encourage them to think about the children in the story, and whether the text shows that they like to hear stories about their grandad. **Award 1 mark for the correct answer ticked.** Skill: Prediction.

Grandad Mandela, by Zazi, Ziwelene and Zindzi Mandela

What do you know about your grandparents? How about your great-grandparents? Did any of them stand up for something that they believed in? Imagine if your great-grandfather was one of the most famous people in history, just like the children in this extract. What would you want to ask him?

One day, Zazi and Ziwelene were playing at Grandma Zindzi's house when they found a photograph. It was someone they remembered very well.

"Look, Grandma!" said Zazi. "We found a picture of Grandad Mandela. Can you tell us about him again?"

"Of course," Grandma Zindzi replied. "As you know, Grandad Mandela was my father, but he went to jail when I was only eighteen months old."

"Why did Grandad go to jail?" asked Zazi.

"He went to jail because he was fighting against apartheid. Apartheid was a law in South Africa that separated black people and white people, and said that white people were better. Grandad was fighting for us all to be equal.

"You know like we say, 'I Love You Lots Like Jelly Tots'? We are different colours but we all taste the same?"

"Uh-huh," said Zazi.

"That's what Grandad Mandela was fighting for."

From *Grandad Mandela* by Zindzi, Zazi and Ziwelene Mandela, published by Frances Lincoln Ltd, copyright © 2018. Reproduced by permission of Frances Lincoln Ltd, an imprint of The Quarto Group.

Word meaning

Name: _____

1 Find and copy **one** word that means 'the same'.

_____

1 mark

2 Which word from the story means the opposite of 'forgotten'? Tick **one**.

remembered ☐

separate ☐

against ☐

law ☐

1 mark

3 *"Can you tell us about him again?"*
Which word in this sentence tells us that the children have already heard the story?

_____

1 mark

4 The author uses the word *separated*. What does it mean?

_____

1 mark

Mix it up!

Name: _____

1 Why did Grandad Mandela go to jail?

_____ 1 mark

2 Which of these events happened first? Tick **one**.

The children asked their grandma to tell them the story of their grandad. ☐

The children were playing. ☐

The children found a photograph of Grandad Mandela. ☐

Grandma Zindzi told the children the story of Grandad Mandela. ☐

1 mark

3 Find and copy **one** sentence that tells us the children knew who was in the photograph.

_____ 1 mark

4 What do you think Zazi and Ziwelene will do next? Tick **one**.

ask more questions about Grandad Mandela's life ☐

eat some jelly sweets ☐

fight with each other ☐

1 mark

Bee Frog

by Martin Waddell

▽ **Printable text**   📖 **Photocopiable text and questions** • pages 169 to 171

Bee Frog is the story of a frog whose parents are too busy to listen to her, so she hops away to pretend to be a dragon. This story is written by Martin Waddell, the author of *Can't You Sleep, Little Bear?* (Unit 6). After enjoying both texts with your class, you could discuss the similarities and differences between them. For guidance on running this task, see page 11.

Progress check questions mark scheme

	Answer	Guidance
1	small ✓	Explain that this is a word meaning question and encourage the children to identify the key words. Then ask them to find and highlight the possible answers in the text and reread the sentences that contain them. Encourage them to notice that two answers come up lots of times. Think aloud: *'Bee' and 'frog' are used for the character's name. They do not mean the same as 'little', so neither of these is the answer.* Remind them to tick one answer only. **Award 1 mark for the correct answer.** Skill: Word meaning.
2	a dragon	Point out that this is a retrieval question and encourage the children to identify the key words. If necessary, think aloud: *When we pretend, we imagine we are something we are not. What animal does Bee Frog say she is to her mum, dad and grandma?* **Award 1 mark for the correct answer.** Skill: Retrieval.
3	Bee Frog played games with her sisters and brothers. [1] Grandma Frog was asleep. [4] Dad Frog told Bee Frog to be quiet. [3] Bee Frog hopped off. [5] Bee Frog told her mum she was a dragon. [2]	Explain to the children that this is a sequencing question. Encourage them to identify the key words in the question and to find, highlight and number each event in the text before filling in the answer boxes. If necessary, think aloud: *First Bee Frog played with her sisters and brothers, so this is number 1.* Repeat for the other events. **Award 1 mark for the correct numbers in at least two boxes. Award 2 marks for the correct numbers in all boxes.** Skill: Sequencing.
4	I think Bee Frog felt lonely. *OR* Bee felt worried/upset/scared about being alone.	Point out to the children that this is an inference question and encourage them to identify the key words. Prompt them to use the locator and focus on the last two lines. If necessary, think aloud: *If I was on my own, I would feel lonely, even if I was a dragon. Bee Frog asks if dragons get lonely. I think she is thinking about this because she is feeling lonely.* **Award 1 mark for any reference to Bee feeling lonely/worried. Do not accept answers that just repeat the text, as this does not make Bee's feelings explicit.** Skill: Inference.
5	Bee Frog will find her family. ✓	Explain that this is a prediction question and encourage the children to identify the key words. You could ask them to think about the endings of other stories they know, or to think about what would happen if their parents realised they were missing. Remind them to tick one answer only. **Award 1 mark for the correct answer ticked.** Skill: Prediction.

Progress check 1

Name: _____

1 Which word from the story means the same as 'little'? Tick **one**.

frog ☐

small ☐

nice ☐

bee ☐

1 mark

2 What did Bee Frog pretend to be?

_____

1 mark

3 Number the events to show the order in which they happened in the story. One has been done for you.

Bee Frog played games with her sisters and brothers. ☐ 1

Grandma Frog was asleep. ☐

Dad Frog told Bee to be quiet. ☐

Bee Frog hopped off. ☐

Bee Frog told her mum she was a dragon. ☐

2 marks

4 How do you think Bee Frog felt at the end of the story?

_____

5 What do you think will happen at the end of the story? Tick **one**.

Bee Frog will find her family. ☐

Bee Frog will turn into a dragon. ☐

1 mark

Bee Frog, by Martin Waddell

Have you ever tried to talk to someone and they haven't responded? How did it make you feel? Why might the other person not have been listening? What did you do when they didn't listen? This text is from a story about a little frog who pretends to be a dragon, but nobody listens to her.

There once was a frog,
a very small frog,
called Bee Frog.

Bee played all day with her sisters and brothers.
They played Can't Catch Me, Frog,
Frog-Hop and
Frog-Plop and …
I'm Not a Frog,
I'm a
DRAGON.
Then Mum Frog called them in.

"I'm Bee Frog the Dragon,"
Bee told Mum Frog.
"Yes, Bee, that's nice,"
croaked Mum Frog.
"I'm not nice, I'm a dragon," croaked Bee.
"Yes, dear, I see," croaked Mum Frog.

"I'm Bee Dragon,"
Bee told Dad Frog.
"Be quiet, Bee," croaked Dad Frog.
"I'm a very fierce dragon!" croaked Bee.
"So I see," said Dad, without looking at Bee.

"I'm Bee Dragon,"
Bee told Grandma Frog.
But Grandma Frog was fast asleep on her lily
and she didn't hear Bee.

"No one listens to me!"
croaked Bee Frog.
"I'm hopping off!"
croaked Bee Frog.

"I'm hopping off
and I'm not coming back,
not ever,
not never!"

Hop, hop, hop, hop, hop, hop, hop.

Bee Frog landed on a dark stone,
with reeds all around it.
I'm Bee Dragon! thought Bee.
I'm Bee Dragon, the really fierce dragon! thought Bee.
Everyone's SCARED of Bee Dragon!
thought Bee.

Then ...
I wonder if Dragons get lonely? thought Bee.

You Can't Take an Elephant on the Bus
by Patricia Cleveland-Peck

▽ **Printable text**   ▭ **Photocopiable text and questions** • **pages 173 to 175**

The children are sure to enjoy this funny rhyming story. In this extract, we learn why certain animals do not make good travel companions. Once the Progress check has been completed, you could discuss it alongside Units 11 and 12. For guidance on running this task, see page 11.

Progress check questions mark scheme

	Answer	Guidance
1	⬭ panic ⬭	Explain that this is a word meaning question and encourage the children to identify the key words. They should then highlight the possible answers in the text and reread the relevant sentences. If necessary, think aloud: *The first word in the list is 'pain'. Pain means that something hurts. That is not the same as fear.* Repeat for the remaining words. Remind the children to circle one answer only. **Award 1 mark for the correct answer ticked.** **Skill: Word meaning.**
2	They would snatch your shopping. ✓	Point out that this is a retrieval question and encourage the children to highlight the key words and use them to scan for the relevant part of the text. If necessary, discuss the possible answers (e.g. *'They would cause a terrible fuss' – this part of the text is about the elephant, so it can't be the answer*). Remind the children to tick one answer only. **Award 1 mark for the correct answer ticked.** **Skill: Retrieval.**
3	an elephant on the bus [1] a seal driving a taxi [4] a tiger travelling by train [3] a centipede on roller skates [5] a monkey sitting in a shopping trolley [2]	Remind the children that this is a sequencing question. Encourage them to identify the key words in the question and to find, highlight and number each animal in the text before filling in the answer boxes. If necessary, think aloud: *The first animal that is mentioned is an elephant, so that is number 1.* Repeat for the remaining animals. **Award 1 mark for the correct numbers in at least two boxes. Award 2 marks for the correct numbers in all boxes.** **Skill: Sequencing.**
4	He would get angry at how long it takes to put skates on his one hundred feet.	Explain to the children that this is an inference question and encourage them to identify the key words. Prompt them to use the locator and find the last verse. If necessary, discuss what 'rage' means. Think aloud: *It is fun to skate and it is quick to put a pair of skates on … oh, but a centipede has 100 feet. How long would it take him to put on 100 skates?* **Award 1 mark for any reference to the centipede having 100 feet and taking a long time to put on 100 skates.** **Skill: Inference.**
5	They will travel in a funny way.	Point out to the children that this is a prediction question. Ask them to think about all the ways in which the animals have travelled so far – are they funny or sensible? Think aloud: *I think the author wants to make us laugh so the animals will keep travelling in funny ways.* Remind them to tick one answer only. **Award 1 mark for the correct answer ticked.** **Skill: Prediction.**

Progress check 2

Name: _____

1 Which word from the story means the same as 'fear'? Circle **one**.

| pain | panic | rage | temper |

1 mark

2 Look at the second verse. Why should you not put a monkey in a shopping trolley? Tick **one**.

They would cause a terrible fuss. ☐

They would spring and leap. ☐

They could not grasp the wheel. ☐

They would snatch your shopping. ☐

1 mark

3 Number the sentences to show the order in which the animals appear in the story. One has been done for you.

an elephant on the bus — 1

a seal driving a taxi ☐

a tiger travelling by train ☐

a centipede on roller skates ☐

a monkey sitting in a shopping trolley ☐

2 marks

4 Look at the last verse. Why would a centipede get in a rage?

_____

_____

1 mark

5 How do you think the animal in the next verse of the story will choose to travel? Tick **one**.

They will travel in a funny way. ☐

They will travel in a sensible way. ☐

1 mark

Photocopiable resource from *Complete Comprehension 1* © Schofield & Sims Ltd, 2020.

You Can't Take an Elephant on the Bus, by Patricia Cleveland-Peck

Have you ever been on a bus? What about in a taxi or on skates? How else have you travelled? Have you ever seen an elephant on a bus? What about a giraffe on an aeroplane? This text comes from a funny rhyming story all about how some silly animals try to travel!

You can't take an elephant
    on the bus ...

It would simply cause
    a terrible fuss!

Elephants' bottoms are
    heavy and fat,

and would certainly squash
    the seats quite flat.

And don't sit a monkey in
    a shopping trolley ...

For monkeys are naughty
    and find it jolly

to snatch your shopping
    and chuck it about.

No, leave monkey at home
    when you go out.

Nor should a tiger travel by train ...

Think of the panic. Think of the pain.

Tigers are built to spring and to leap.

Think of the passengers half-asleep.

And don't hail a taxi if the driver's a seal ...

With such slippery flippers, he can't grasp the wheel.

The taxi will slither and probably swerve,

then throw everyone out at the very next curve.

A centipede on roller skates is rather bizarre ...

With one hundred feet, he'd go fast and go far.

But to put on his boots would take him an age –

he'd get in a temper, he'd get in a rage.

From *You Can't Take an Elephant on the Bus* © Patricia Cleveland-Peck, 2015, Bloomsbury Publishing Plc.

Progress check 3

Seaside Towns
by Claire Hibbert

▽ **Printable text** • **Modelling slides**   📖 **Photocopiable text and questions** • **pages 177 to 179**

This information text provides facts about coastal towns in the UK, exploring the different kinds of building found on beaches and the activities that can be enjoyed at the seaside. The topic links to the Key Stage 1 geography curriculum and could also be linked to Unit 17. For guidance on running this task, see page 11.

Progress check questions mark scheme

	Answer	Guidance
1	lido	Explain that this is a word meaning question and encourage the children to identify the key words. They should then find and highlight the possible answers in the text and reread the relevant sentences. Think aloud: *The text says, 'Beach huts are wooden cabins', and I can see in the picture that they look like little houses, so I know that a beach hut is not the same as an outdoor pool.* Repeat for the remaining answers. Remind the children to circle one answer only. **Award 1 mark for the correct answer ticked.** Skill: Word meaning.
2	so they don't get wet at high tide	Point out that this is a retrieval question and encourage the children to identify the key words. Think aloud: *I need to find the part where it says that beach huts are at the top of the beach.* If necessary, continue: *The text says, 'they won't get wet at high tide'.* **Award 1 mark for the correct answer.** Skill: Retrieval.
3	wood [1] concrete [3] iron [2]	Explain that this is a sequencing question and encourage the children to identify the key words. Prompt them to use the locator to find the right section. They should then find, highlight and number each of the possible answers in the text before filling in the answer boxes. **Award 1 mark for the correct numbers in both boxes.** Skill: Sequencing.
4	because people visit the seaside to have fun	Explain that this is an inference question and encourage the children to identify the key words. Then ask them to think about the purpose of an amusement park. Think aloud: *If I was visiting the seaside, would I be expecting to be bored or to have fun? If it was too cold to play on the beach I could go to the amusement park to have fun.* You could also point out that 'amusement' is another word for 'enjoyment' or 'laughter'. **Award 1 mark for any reference to people visiting seaside towns to enjoy themselves.** Skill: Inference.
5	Sea safety ✓	Point out that this is a prediction question. Ask the children to think about what information would go under each of the possible answers. Which subheading links best to the subject of the comprehension text? Remind them to tick one answer only. **Award 1 mark for the correct answer ticked.** Skill: Prediction.

Progress check 3

Name: _____

1 Which of these words from the text is a different name for an outdoor pool? Circle **one**.

| beach hut | lido | amusement park | pebble |

1 mark

2 Look at the second paragraph. Why are beach huts built at the top of the beach?

_____

1 mark

3 Look at the section **On the seafront**.
Piers have been made out of different materials over the years. Number the materials to show the order in which they were used. One has been done for you.

wood — 1

concrete — ☐

iron — ☐

1 mark

4 Why do you think there are sometimes amusement parks in seaside towns?

_____

1 mark

5 Which other subheading do you think a book about seaside towns might have? Tick **one**.

Dinosaurs ☐

Sea safety ☐

Stars and planets ☐

Your body ☐

1 mark

Seaside Towns, by Claire Hibbert

This text is from a book about seaside towns in the United Kingdom. Have you ever been to the seaside? What was it like? What did you do? If you haven't been, have you seen photographs or film clips of the seaside? What would you like to do there if you visit in the future?

Beach buildings

Seaside towns often have a beach. It might be sandy or covered in shingle (pebbles). There are special buildings on and around the beach.

Beach huts are wooden cabins. They are often pretty colours. They stand at the top of the beach, where they won't get wet at high tide. People get changed in their beach hut before they sunbathe or swim in the sea. They use the hut to store deck chairs, blankets and beach toys.

There are other useful buildings on the beach. Kiosks sell drinks and snacks. There are public toilets and showers. Some beaches have an outdoor pool called a lido. The lido is a safer, warmer place to swim and play than the sea.

On the seafront

Many seaside towns have a pier. It is a walkway that sticks out into the sea. The first piers were made of wood. Later, iron was used and then concrete.

People visit piers to have fun. There are cafes and stalls and lots of games to play. There might even be fairground rides for children. Some seaside towns have big amusement parks with rides for all the family.

From *Seaside Towns* by Claire Hibbert. Reproduced by permission of Franklin Watts, an imprint of Hachette Children's Books, Carmelite House, 50 Victoria Embankment, London, EC4Y 0DZ.

Discover *Complete Comprehension* for Year 2

Unit	Target skill	Title	Author	Genre
1	Retrieval	Lions, Lions, Lions	Laura Lodge	Non-fiction
2	Inference	There's a Lion in My Cornflakes	Michelle Robinson	Fiction
3	Retrieval	The Great Fire of London	Emma Adams	Non-fiction
4	Retrieval	Guy Fawkes	Laura Lodge	Non-fiction
5	Word meaning	Eight Candles Burning	Celia Warren	Poetry
6	Retrieval	Christmas Eve	Brian Moses	Poetry
Progress check 1	Mixed skills	Ruby's Worry	Tom Percival	Fiction
7	Inference	Perfectly Norman	Tom Percival	Fiction
8	Sequencing	Sir Charlie Stinky Socks: The Really Big Adventure	Kristina Stephenson	Fiction
9	Inference	The Night Dragon	Naomi Howarth	Fiction
10	Retrieval	How to Build a Gingerbread House	Laura Lodge	Non-fiction
11	Retrieval	Hansel and Gretel	Laura Lodge	Fiction
12	Inference	Hansel and Gretel	Bethan Woollvin	Fiction
Progress check 2	Mixed skills	The Life of Roald Dahl: A Marvellous Adventure	Emma Fischel	Non-fiction
13	Retrieval	George's Marvellous Medicine	Roald Dahl	Fiction
14	Prediction	Horrid Henry and the Football Fiend	Francesca Simon	Fiction
15	Word meaning	The Hundred-Mile-An-Hour Dog	Jeremy Strong	Fiction
16	Word meaning	The Darkest Dark	Chris Hadfield	Fiction
17	Retrieval	Dogs in Space	Vix Southgate	Non-fiction
18	Inference	A Bottle of Happiness	Pippa Goodheart	Fiction
Progress check 3	Mixed skills	Ossiri and the Bala Mengro	Richard O'Neill and Katharine Quarmby	Fiction

Schofield & Sims

For further information and to place your order visit www.schofieldandsims.co.uk or telephone 01484 607080